Puffin Books
Editor: Kaye Webb

Something to Collect

If you've got more than two or three special matchboxes, buttons, old tin cans, cigarette cards, bus tickets or holiday souvenirs you are well on the way to being a 'collector'

And you can build up a collection of almost *anything*. (Someone once decided to collect the tissue-paper wrappings from oranges, and *that* collection is now in the Victoria & Albert Museum, London.) In this book the authors show you how you can go about making a worthwhile collection of what interests you. There is advice on how to preserve and display different kinds of collections, where to find further items, how to find out more about particular subjects, and information on specialist clubs, societies, books and museum collections.

The authors have concentrated on cheap and easy-to-find collectable objects, both natural and manufactured, and if you aren't a collector when you pick up this book, you will be before long!

Mary Norwak and
Sue Gibson

Something
to Collect

Puffin Books

Puffin Books,
Penguin Books Ltd, Harmondsworth,
Middlesex, England
Penguin Books, 625 Madison Avenue,
New York, New York 10022, U.S.A.
Penguin Books Australia Ltd, Ringwood,
Victoria, Australia
Penguin Books Canada Ltd, 2801 John Street,
Markham, Ontario, Canada L3R 1B4
Penguin Books (N.Z.) Ltd, 182–190 Wairau Road,
Auckland 10, New Zealand

First published by Pelham Books 1976

Published in Puffin Books 1978

Made and printed in Great Britain by
Richard Clay (The Chaucer Press) Ltd
Bungay, Suffolk
Set in 'Monophoto' Times

Contents

Introduction

You may not realize you are already a collector, but if you have two or three similar things, like kinds of buttons or toy soldiers, it shows that you are already starting a collection. In our two families, we collect practically everything because we are like magpies and pick up a lot of things which attract us. We have collections of photographs and postcards, pressed glass, little boxes, badges, pieces of needlework, dolls, model animals, bottles, fossils, fruit wrappers, old games and toys, and many other things besides.

A collector doesn't have to be rich, but he has to give up a little time for collecting, but this won't matter because it is such an interesting hobby. You can never be bored if you are a collector. You will notice all the little things which people have in their houses, you will find unusual shops, visit museums and old houses whether you are at home or abroad, and go to lectures and exhibitions. You will find books about your special subject, and pages in newspapers and magazines. Other people collect the same sort of things, and you often make new friends through this shared interest. Even non-collectors will be excited by your enthusiasm and will start to bring you things for your collection.

If you don't know what to collect, think of the things you are interested in. You can collect items to do with sport, animals, the theatre or ballet, or travel, or you can just collect objects which you find beautiful or unusual. You may have been working on a school project and found the subject stimulated you to find out more so that a collection gradually builds up. Most large towns have a museum, or a library which has small exhibitions, and there are many specialized museums such as those devoted to dolls or transport which you will find interesting. Get hold of a copy of a booklet called *Museums & Galleries in Great Britain & Ireland* (published by ABC Historic Publications) which is revised every year and lists details of all the places you can visit. Look in the library and see all the books which have been written about collections, and about natural history if you want to collect natural objects. Ask in the library if there are any clubs or societies in the area which have meetings and lectures on your special subject, and see if there is a list of magazines written for collectors.

When you start to collect, find what you can for nothing first. You may already have a few things yourself, but ask if your parents, older members of the family and friends have similar things they don't want. Ask for permission to look through drawers, cupboards and old boxes which may have all sorts of hidden treasures from your point of view. From this first kind of collecting, you can go on to look for things at jumble sales and on junk stalls in markets where items can be bought very cheaply; later, you may have enough money to go to a specialist shop or to buy through the advertisement columns of magazines. When your family begin to take an interest in the collection, you may find they will give you rather special things for birthday or Christmas presents, or you can ask them to take you to places for a treat so that you can all see similar collections.

Some people only collect things because they are valuable, but they are not true collectors. A true collector is someone who likes things for their own beauty or interest and not for what they are worth. As you build up a collection, detective work may reveal old or rare items which you find by chance and get hold of cheaply or which perhaps the family may one day buy for you if they are more expensive. Some things like cigarette cards, postcards, photographs and dolls have started to become much sought after, and some varieties are rare and expensive. Don't let this put you off if you are interested in the subject, but don't be tempted to buy expensive things. Collect cheaply and keep an eye on catalogues and current values and you may find you have something special.

Enjoy your collecting, and you may soon find you become an expert on something quite unusual. Quite independently, a handful of people have collected the thin papers wrapped round oranges because they are so pretty. Some fine collections have been built up and these have now been given to the Victoria & Albert Museum in London, who have designed a special information chart about them. This is a good example of a collection of interesting objects which cost nothing but gradually grew in interest until it achieved museum status, as did another collection of biscuit tins and one of small household objects made in wood. We have tried to avoid the specialized subjects like stamps, about which much has been written, but just look through this book and you will be surprised at some of the things which we have found people enjoy collecting.

Displaying a collection

A collection isn't much fun if you just tuck everything away in a muddle in boxes or cupboards. Your collection should be interesting, and sometimes beautiful, and it will improve greatly if carefully classified and arranged with neatness and order. You may quickly work out your own favourite method of showing a collection for your own pleasure and other people's interest, but here are some useful suggestions.

Paper items, and some flat objects such as badges or needlework, and some natural objects are best kept flat. They can be mounted in scrapbooks, which should be large and firm, or on large cards which can be punched and bound together. (Loose-leaf or exercise books are usually too flimsy for good display unless they have thin card pages.) You can also use index cards kept in a filing box or drawer, or put larger items straight into a box file or folder to save sticking down. There are special albums for postcards, photographs, cigarette cards and such like, or you can make your own, using slits or special mounting corners instead of glue. If you like to have things where they can be seen easily, put some of your collection on pinboards covered with felt, or on cork tiles which can be stuck on to a wall to make a noticeboard, then things can be changed regularly and easily. If you only collect paper things or natural objects for their decorative value, you can use them to cover screens or wastepaper baskets, or to make into pictures and collages. Some things, like cloth badges, can be sewn on to curtains, bedcovers or cushions to make an attractive display.

A cutlery box can be turned on its side to display small objects

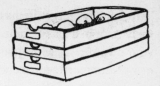

Filing trays are useful for pebbles and shells

A screen is a useful way of showing paper items neatly

A pinboard can be made of cork or felt-covered hardboard

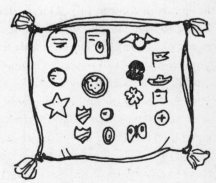

Badges can be sewn or pinned on a plain cushion

If you have larger items to display, they can be shown on open shelves, or in a glass-fronted cabinet to avoid dust. You can make your own shelves with shoe-boxes or wooden boxes on their sides, or with compartmented cutlery boxes for smaller items. These can also be flat on shelves or tables. A lot of small things can be arranged in small chests of drawers which have been used as specimen cabinets, or in stationery or filing cabinets. Seed trays and letter trays make very good display cabinets and they can be covered with transparent film to prevent items getting dusty. Of course, some of your collection can be used regularly in your room or house, if it is something like glass, but this may mean damage, and it is safest to keep your most precious things in a special place to be looked at and studied.

Natural objects

Feathers

It is possible to find feathers in all sorts of places. You may find pigeon feathers in towns, sea-bird feathers on the beach, river-bird feathers in parks, and of course all sorts of feathers in the garden or on a country walk. Even canary or parrot feathers are interesting. There are usually more feathers about in the early autumn when birds are moulting.

Look at a good bird book or at charts issued by the Royal Society for the Protection of Birds to see which bird and which part of the body your feathers come from. The feathers can be mounted in a scrapbook or on stiff sheets of paper with thin strips of gummed paper or tape. Include the name of the bird and the date and place you found the feathers. If you have some small feathers, they can be mounted on microscope slide glasses so you can study them carefully.

Once you start to collect feathers, you will soon want to know more about the birds which have shed them. You can start by becoming a bird-watcher, and this doesn't mean going a long way to find the birds. If you have a nest-box or a bird table in the garden, you can already see many different kinds of birds. Even without these, you will find that some birds like special plants and shrubs in the garden, or thick hedges and trees, and it is worth keeping a record of the birds which visit regularly.

If you become really interested in bird life, write to the Royal Society for the Protection of Birds, The Lodge, Sandy, Bedfordshire, who have all sorts of books and charts available,

Jay feather

Turkey feather

Owl feather

and suggestions for attracting birds to your garden. The Society runs the Young Ornithologists' Club which has its own magazine, and runs projects, outings and holidays connected with birds.

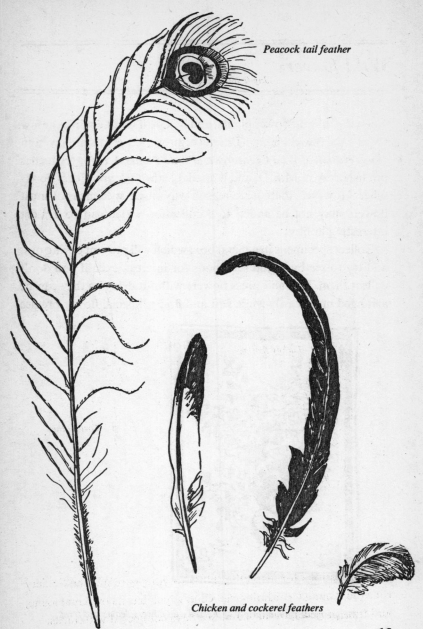

Peacock tail feather

Chicken and cockerel feathers

Wild flowers

Never dig up wild flower plants, and be sure it is not against the law to pick the flowers either. Details of protected plants are given in *Conservation of Wild Creatures and Wild Plants Act, 1975,* which is published by H.M.S.O. and is available through your local bookseller. However, there is no reason why single specimens of most flowers may not be added to a collection which can be a most interesting hobby.

Collect specimens in a metal box, which will prevent drying out, and try to see buds and seed pods for interest, even if you don't collect them. Dry and press flowers without delay as they can be arranged more easily while soft and fleshy. Special flower presses

Picture made from a variety of pressed wild flowers, leaves and ferns

can be bought cheaply, consisting of sheets of blotting paper and board pressed between wooden boards which can be screwed tightly together. If you haven't a special press, use heavy books for weight and plenty of blotting paper. Carefully arrange the flowers on blotting paper with a small paintbrush, and press with more

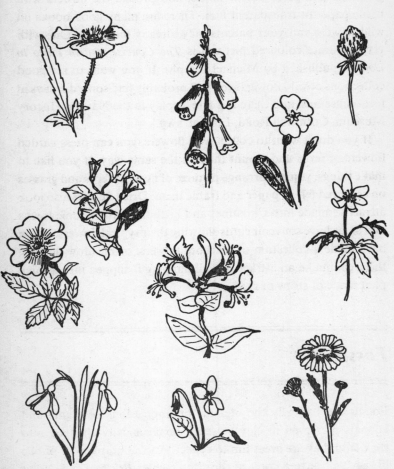

Some of the most common wild flowers showing the wide variety of shape and leaf which can be combined to make attractive pictures

blotting paper under weight. Re-press in fresh paper after two days and press for four days altogether (some large flowers may need longer).

Mount your specimens on thick paper or cards, using thin strips of sticky paper or tape across the stems. Identify the flowers and give date and place on the labels, and protect the flowers with tissue paper or transparent film. There are many good books on wild flowers and your parents may already have one. One with very accurate coloured pictures is *The Concise British Flora in Colour* (published by Michael Joseph). If you want to see good collections of wild flowers, you will probably find some displays in local museums, and there is a fine display in the Natural History Museum, Cromwell Road, London sw7.

If you don't want to collect wild flowers, you can press garden flowers or ferns and mount them in the same way. If you like to make things, you can arrange pictures of flowers, ferns and grasses on coloured felt or paper and frame them. Dried flowers also look attractive made into Christmas and birthday cards – some towns and areas have souvenir cards showing their typical flowers. If you have made a collection of seashore flowers, or meadow flowers, these can make an attractive wall hanging if slipped into a thick plait made of straw or reed.

Fossils

Fossils are basically the remains or impressions of plants and animals preserved in clay or sand, or chemically changed into rock, and they are great fun to collect. A local museum or public library will have a copy of the *Directory of British Fossiliferous Localities* which will give you an idea where to start hunting. Fossils can be found in woods and sandbanks, in rocks and cliffs, on beaches and in quarries, but you must be very careful where you hunt, and must have permission to visit places such as quarries which have been excavated.

Fossils do not occur in all kinds of rock, for instance they are not found in granite. Limestone, chalk or clay are the best places to look, and you can find these areas marked on a geological map of your area. You will need a little equipment for fossil-hunting – just a hammer and chisel, and a bag to carry the fossils. It is also a good idea to carry a small notebook so you can record exactly where you found the fossils, and be sure to wear old clothes as fossil-hunting is dirty. To remove a fossil, you need to put the chisel edge on the rock just above it and hit the chisel gently with a hammer, and you will knock off a piece of rock a little bigger than the fossil.

There are some very exciting fossils to be found of course, such as prints of prehistoric animals, but even without chiselling them out you can find a lot of small fossils on the ground. Some of the most common are ammonites which are seasnail shells, and these can be tiny or very large indeed. There are also bullet-shaped belemnites a few inches long which are the fossilized bones of extinct cuttle fish. 'Devil's toenails' are the ends of big tough oyster shells curled up like the nails on an animal's foot. These are often found in fields, as are fossilized sea urchins which look like ordinary stones until you see the sea urchin markings on them.

Coral and fossil sharks' teeth

A variety of fossil shells

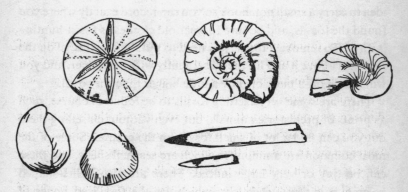

(Top) *Sea urchin, ammonite and 'devil's toenail'*
(Bottom) *Brachiopods and belemnites*

Leaf and seeds in shale, and fossil wood

Many museums have a collection of geological finds, and you may like to visit the Science Museum, Exhibition Road, London sw7, to learn more. The Lyme Regis area of Dorset is particularly famous for its fossils. A very detailed book on the subject is *The Little Guide to Fossils* (published by Paul Hamlyn).

Grasses

The grass family is the largest and most important family of flowering plants in Britain, and it includes the cereals grown for food, grasses for hay and grazing, and more than 150 wild species. You will of course find grasses in cultivated fields, but must never damage growing crops. It is better to look for the wild grasses which grow along the hedgerows and verges; some species grow better on marshland, and there are many kinds which grow best by the sea, and still more which prefer chalk and limestone soils.

Most wild flower books include grasses and there are plenty of illustrations from which you can identify them. Identification is made from the heads of the grasses which contain thousands of small flowers and seeds, and the best time to collect them is summer, although dried grass can be found throughout the year. These dried grasses look attractive in pots as a decoration, but it is a good idea to stick the stems into modelling clay to keep them upright. You may need a magnifying glass or microscope to study the grasses properly and you will find dozens of different kinds. As well as using them for decoration, try pressing the grasses between blotting paper and weights (see Wild flowers). Mount them in a book with their identifying names, and the date and place they were found.

If you are particularly interested in the grasses which are grown for food, such as wheat, barley, oats and rye, you can find out more about these grains from the Flour Advisory Bureau, 21 Arlington Street, London W1. You may have a local miller who can show you the different kinds of grain grown in Europe and in America and Canada. Some brewers can help you with information about the barley used for brewing, and breakfast cereal manufacturers will tell you about oats and maize. There is useful information on grasses in the *AA Book of the Countryside*.

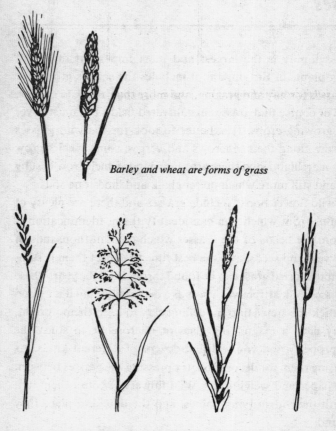

Barley and wheat are forms of grass

Couch-grass, tufted hair-grass, marram and cord-grass

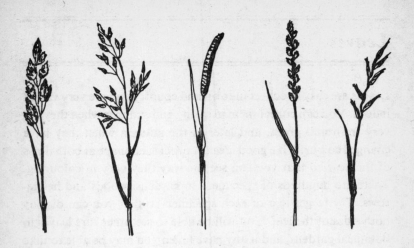

Cocksfoot, tall fescue, timothy-grass, rye-grass and tor-grass

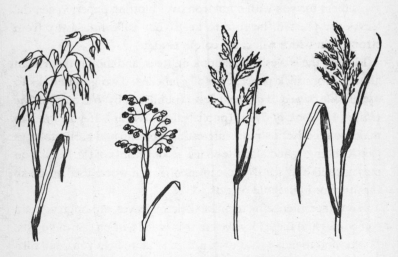

Wild oats, quaking-grass, reed-canary and common reed-grass

Leaves

Leaves are easy to collect in town and country and are very varied indeed. You can collect them in spring and summer when they are very fresh and green, and later in the autumn when they have changed colour. It is a good idea to collect each shape at both times of the year so that you can see the way they vary in colouring. There are hundreds of specimens in gardens. woods and hedgerows. Try to get two of each specimen so that you can display both sides of the leaf. You will be able to see other rare leaves in botanical gardens, and if any have fallen you may be able to take them, but it may be as well to ask a keeper or gardener before doing so.

Press the leaves in the same way as wild flowers between blotting paper and weights. They usually take less time than flowers as they are not so moist. If you want to dry them quickly, ask someone to press them for you with a hot iron over blotting paper. When the leaves are pressed, be sure to keep your collection away from strong light which will cause colour change.

Identify the leaves from a book on trees, and mount them in an album or on thick paper, carefully labelled. Two good books to use are *Wayside & Woodland Trees* (published by Warne) and *The Observer's Book of Trees* (published by Warne). If you want to make your collection more interesting, you can add bark rubbings (see Rubbings), and also the cones, seeds or nuts of the trees. You may also like to see if you can identify the wood used to make furniture or household objects.

It is rather interesting to make skeleton leaves, although you can sometimes find these lacy skeletons in woods, or on sale in florists. If you want to make your own, ask an adult to help you. Half fill a saucepan with water and add a tablespoon of washing soda for

24

A skeleton leaf shows the pattern of tiny veins

every litre (1¾ pints) of water. Heat it until nearly boiling, and then put in the leaves. Simmer gently for an hour, and then cool.

Brush the leaves gently with a nail-brush to remove the softened flesh and leave the lacy skeleton. Put the skeleton leaves into a little bleach for an hour and then let them rinse gently under a cold water tap. Blot the skeletons gently under blotting paper before mounting them or arranging them as decorations.

Oak, ash and beech leaves and seeds

Horse chestnut, sweet chestnut and sycamore

Yew, holly and Norwegian spruce

Skeletons and bones

If you have ever found a small skeleton, or a collection of odd bones in the garden, you may have spent some time trying to find out something about them and where they came from. If you search around, you may soon find more, and you can begin to build up a picture of the place in which they are found.

In the garden or in the fields you can often find jawbones or larger skulls of cattle and horses, often complete with teeth. In areas where there is parkland and woodland, you may find deer bones or skulls, or pieces of antlers. Small skeletons and skulls which turn up all over the place are rabbits, mice and birds. You may often find small skeletons in sheds or outbuildings, and bird skeletons are common in chimneys. If you live in an old house, you may find small animal skeletons in cupboards or attics.

There are, of course, other kinds of skeletons such as fish which you can find on the seashore. A fishmonger may let you have fish skeletons, and if you want to study larger bones, perhaps the butcher will let you have some.

When you have collected a complete bird or small animal skeleton, it will be very frail and difficult to clean. Lift it on to a pad of cotton wool or paper to carry home and try to keep the bones in their natural position. If you really want to clean them, brush the skeleton gently with a small soft paintbrush. Larger bones and skulls can be cleaned and brushed with warm soapy water. You will probably be able to identify the bones from the place where they were found, so don't forget to label them carefully. You will probably need a series of boxes to keep them in. Cover the boxes with transparent film so they keep clean and can remain undisturbed.

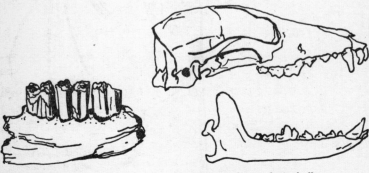

Jawbone complete with teeth   *Two parts from a dog's skull*

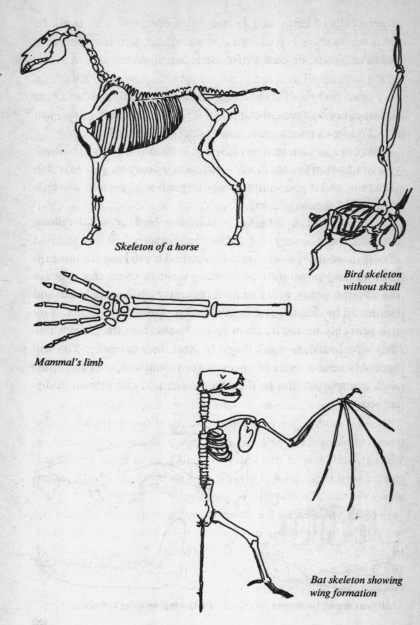

Skeleton of a horse

Bird skeleton
without skull

Mammal's limb

Bat skeleton showing
wing formation

Rocks, minerals and pebbles

All sorts of everyday materials are really rocks, such as coal, granite, marble and flint, but there are hundreds of other fascinating ones. Some can be found in open fields, road workings or on the sides of hills, but the best ones are usually to be found on beaches and in rocky and mountainous areas. If you can possibly visit the Geological Museum in London, or see a collection in a local museum, you will see a fantastic range of different rocks and some very beautiful minerals.

To make your own collection you will need similar equipment to fossil-hunters. Wear old clothes, and take a hammer and a rock- or metal-cutting chisel (a chisel used for wood is not strong enough for the hard work of rock-collecting). The Natural History Museum, Cromwell Road, London sw7, has a leaflet on *Hints for Collectors of Fossils and Rocks,* and the Geological Museum, Exhibition Road, London sw7, sells regional handbooks and maps. Each region has its own characteristic rocks, and you may find specimens of these made into craft objects in local shops.

When you have begun your collection, try to identify the rocks from a book such as *The Observer's Book of Geology* (published by Warne), and classify them according to area or type. Specimens can be very large, so it is a good idea to break them into pieces about the size of a matchbox.

Pebbles are pieces of rock which have been worn smooth by weather or by the action of water, and you have probably picked up many pretty ones on visits to the seaside. Some pebbles are in fact semi-precious stones such as amethyst, carnelian or onyx, and can be made into jewellery.

If you want to know more about the pebbles you have found,

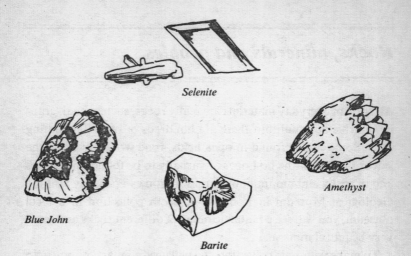

Selenite

Blue John

Barite

Amethyst

read *Pebbles on the Beach* (published by Faber & Faber) which gives plenty of pictures to help identification, and which tells you the areas in which different types of pebble are found.

Take a bag with you when you visit a beach and look very carefully for the kind of stones you want. A good place to look is where the sea has just gone out and the sun is glinting on the wet pebbles as this will show up any translucent ones such as carnelian. It is always a good idea to look on the beach after a storm as the pebbles have been greatly disturbed and millions of new ones thrown up in places you may have inspected regularly before.

If you join a club (ask at the library if there is one in your area), you will be able to compare your collection, perhaps swop stones, and share equipment for the professional polishing and cutting of pebbles.

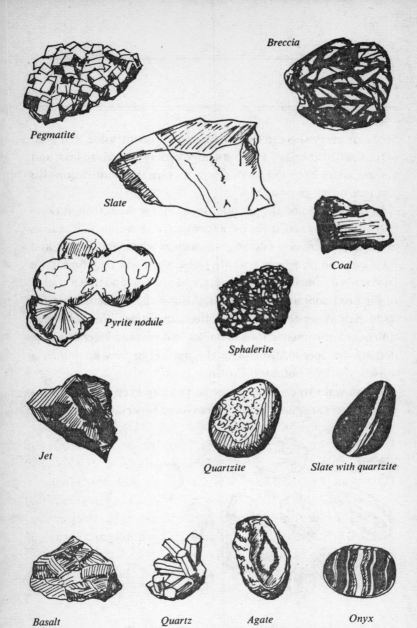

Pegmatite

Breccia

Slate

Coal

Pyrite nodule

Sphalerite

Jet

Quartzite

Slate with quartzite

Basalt

Quartz

Agate

Onyx

Seeds

Seeds are everywhere in the garden and the countryside, and even in the kitchen at home. There is a huge variety of seeds to find, and you can either keep and catalogue them, turn them into decorative pictures, or try growing them.

In the garden and the country, look out for seeds from flowers and vegetables, and from trees (conkers, beech-nuts and acorns are seeds). There is of course grain such as wheat and barley, and the seeds and pips from fruit. In the kitchen you may find more fruit seeds like melon pips and nuts, and you will find that a packet of birdseed contains many kinds. Also in the kitchen, there are such seeds as pepper, mustard, coffee and nutmeg. For identification of unknown seeds, look in books on flowers and trees, and see if there are special displays in the natural history section of a museum, or in a botanical garden.

If you want to classify the seeds, you can keep them in boxes (matchboxes are good) or stick them on to paper. If you have a lot

A collection of birdseeds including sunflowers, maize and peanuts

Kitchen seeds including cloves, nutmegs and coffee beans

of seeds, they can be mounted with transparent glue to make lovely collages, or to make patterns on boxes. Some people like to thread seeds to make necklaces. A book called *Seed Picture Making* (published by Blandford Press) is all about seed collages.

If you want to grow your seeds, try growing them by the jam-jar method. Line a jar with damp kitchen paper or blotting paper and put several seeds between it and the glass. Keep an inch of water in the bottom of the jar, and you will soon see each seed growing a shoot and a root. Apple pips and plum stones grow better if put between pads of cotton wool and placed in a jar in the refrigerator for two months, keeping the cotton wool damp. In warm places, you can grow orange pips, peach stones, melons and cucumbers. A really helpful book about growing seeds is *The Pip Book* (published by Witherby and in Penguin, 1977).

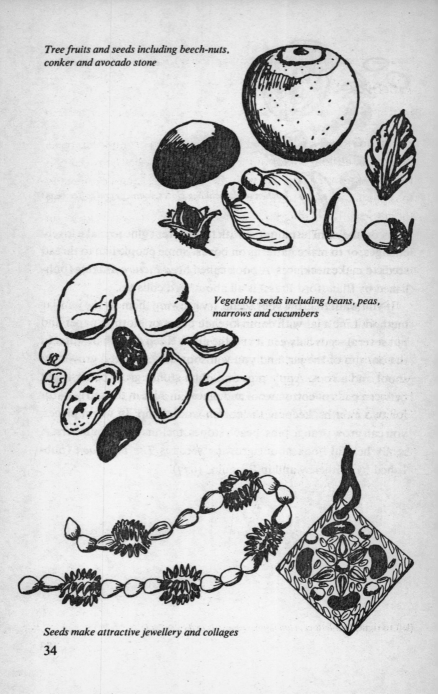

Tree fruits and seeds including beech-nuts, conker and avocado stone

Vegetable seeds including beans, peas, marrows and cucumbers

Seeds make attractive jewellery and collages

Seaweeds

About 700 species of seaweed have been found around the coasts of Britain, although a lot of them look very similar. Seaweed collections were very popular with the Victorians, and if you enjoy looking at their interesting and pretty shapes, you will not find them too difficult to collect on holiday. Most seaweeds grow on rocks or shells, or on other seaweeds, and you do not find many large seaweeds on shingle or sandy beaches because the waves move the pieces and prevent the spores of the larger seaweeds from developing.

Botanists divide seaweeds into greens, browns and reds, but some of the colour variations can look quite different, and colour drains from seaweeds when they are torn away from their living place by storms or when they die and bleach. They are not easy to identify because so many kinds look alike, but it is easier to identify them if large pieces are used. A good book on all sea objects is Collins's *Pocket Guide to the Seashore*.

(left to right) *Sea-lettuce, cladophora rupestris and intestinals*

When you have collected your seaweeds, you will want to keep and mount them. Float the seaweed in slightly salted water and underneath it slide the piece of paper you want to mount it on. Underneath this put a flat tray and then lift up the tray and paper and let the water run off. Put the paper and seaweed between sheets of blotting paper with weights on top (see also Wild flowers) and leave until completely dry.

Pieces of finished seaweed can be mounted in an album, or on white filing cards, with the name of the seaweed, and the place and date on which you found it. If you are more interested in the beautiful appearance of the seaweed than in its botanical classification, try arranging the seaweeds into a collage, sticking each piece with a little transparent glue. Decorative seaweed albums and pictures were very popular in Victorian times, and some of the pictures included tiny shells and dried sea creatures too.

(left to right) *Chondrus crispus, purple laver and dulse*

Coral weed and ahafeltia plicata

36

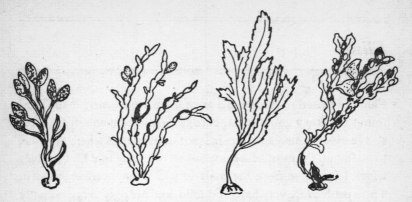

(left to right) *Channelled-wrack, knotted-wrack, serrated-wrack and bladder-wrack*

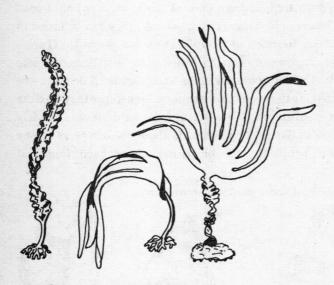

(left to right) *Sea-belt, tangles and furbelows*

Flints

Flint is a material which had a great influence on early man. They found that they could make hard, sharp implements from flint, and early settlements were made in the chalklands where flint was to be found. On most beaches, you can of course find flint pebbles which have come from the chalk in which they were embedded. These pebbles are very hard and solid, and are only very gradually worn down by the action of the sea from their original rough, sharp state into smooth round pebbles. The fragments which are worn off are gradually ground down into sand.

Inland, flints are found in a mass of chalk, either in continuous bands or layers or in lumps, or occasionally they can be found in clay soil. Near Brandon in Norfolk, there is a site called Grimes Graves which you can visit. This was an early settlement where men worked underground in caves and tunnels to dislodge the flints for making their tools and weapons. Sometimes they used the antlers of deer as picks to work out the hard stones. Crudely shaped tools of flint which were made about 400,000 years ago by the earliest people to inhabit Britain have been found at

Naturally formed flint cutting tool

Hand axes shaped from flints

Flint arrowheads which were bound on to wood and (right) *pointed flint lance head*

Natural flint before working

Neolithic axe head

Swanscombe in the Thames Valley. This kind of tool, which is found mainly in Essex, Kent, Suffolk and Norfolk, is called an 'eolith', and some are natural flints which have been usefully shaped by the weather. Early man made rough axes by striking flakes from the central core of a stone, leaving one end thick and easy to grasp, and the other pointed. Scrapers and arrowheads were also fashioned, sometimes mounted on wooden handles or those made from antlers. You will see examples of such tools in many museums, and will gradually get to know which flints have been shaped by nature and which by man.

39

Start your collection with stones from the beach, and identify them by looking at a book called *Pebbles on the Beach* (published by Faber & Faber). When you have seen a collection in a museum, you will be able to recognize flints if you pick them up in fields, and may even find some early tools or weapons. Flints were later used for striking sparks in guns, after the flintlock gun was invented in 1612, and these flints are still shaped in Norfolk. In East Anglia, flint was plentiful and used for building houses and churches. Men called flint-knappers shaped the stones with flat shiny surfaces to form whole walls or decorative patterns. You might like to find some drawings or photographs of these buildings to make your collection more interesting.

Cottage faced with flints

Shells

Sea and river shells are beautiful things to collect. You can find them by the seashore or on the river bed, or get them from fishing boats, and even from your local fishmonger. There are shops where you can buy shells, particularly by the sea, and you may even find antique shells which were used for decoration, or as counters for games.

Sea shells are most easily found after a storm when the shoreline has been altered, and there are often plenty of shells around rocks, since some of the creatures which inhabit the shells live on rocks. If a shell still has a living creature in it, you will have to scoop it out. Wash the shells with warm water and a soft brush to clean them.

(left to right) *Razor, scallop and ormer shells*

(from top clockwise) *Flat winkles, tower, banded wedge. Baltic tellin, European cowries and limpet*

Dry them well, and if you like coat with a thin layer of varnish or clear nail varnish. Look them up in a book, and then store them in matchboxes or in shallow trays with identification labels. Good books to study are *Discovering Sea Shells* (published by Shire), and *Your Book of Shell Collecting* (published by Faber & Faber).

If you like the beautiful shape of shells, you might like to use them to cover boxes or furniture, or to make picture or mirror frames, or turn them into flowers, dolls or animals. You will see examples of these on sale in shops at the seaside. The first shell gift shop was on the Old Chain Pier at Brighton in the 1820s and many people liked to have ornate shell ornaments such as flower baskets and cottages in their houses. Small houses were sometimes decorated with shells – there is one in Hatfield Forest, near

(from top clockwise) *Cockles, winkles, whelk, oyster and mussel*

Bishop's Stortford, Herts. Other large houses had grottoes in their gardens or rooms decorated with shells, and there is a room like this at Woburn Abbey. If you want to see a huge collection of shells and things made from them, go to see the Shell Museum, Glandford, Holt, Norfolk.

Cameo picture carved on souvenir shell

Victorian figure made from shells

Paper

Charity flags and stickers

There used to be dozens of flag-days when charities were allowed to collect money in the streets and flags or emblems were given out to show that a person had made a contribution. There are only a few special collections now such as those for Poppy Day, Alexandra Day and Red Cross Week, but many charities still like to issue emblems to indicate their helpers or financial supporters.

A few charities still issue very distinctive badges, like fabric poppies and roses, but most now have paper emblems. You can often find these at home among other paper oddments. Look out for some of the special shapes like geraniums for the blind, or lifeboats. Designs have changed over the years, and you may find that the old pinned paper shapes have given way to sticky labels for clothes which save metal for the pins and also labour for assembly. During the two World Wars, there were many special flag-days to raise money for the war effort or forces' charities. You will sometimes find these and other charity emblems mounted into a collage and framed, or the early fabric ones were used to decorate pin-cushions.

Some charities are not connected with helping the sick or poor, but with some form of conservation, such as the National Trust, World Wildlife Fund or the various naturalists' trusts. They do not have special collections, but issue car stickers, helpers' badges and other souvenirs. As well as these obvious charity emblems, you may find old collecting boxes (see Moneyboxes), posters, collection envelopes or advertising material.

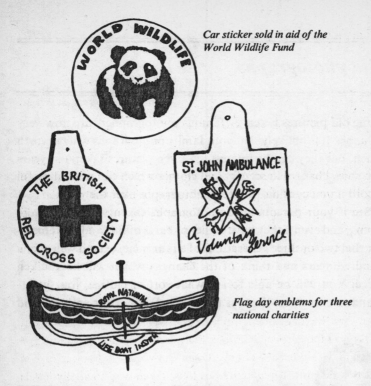

Car sticker sold in aid of the
World Wildlife Fund

Flag day emblems for three
national charities

Emblems can of course be mounted in books, but if you have
plenty of them they look very attractive made into a collage, or
they can be pinned on to a screen or a noticeboard.

Collection envelope distributed by a seamen's charity

Old photographs

Some old pictures taken by famous photographers are now very valuable. It is unlikely that your family photographs will be worth much, but they can be interesting. Even pictures taken ten years ago show changes in scenery and clothes which can make a useful record if you continue to keep photographs over the years.

See if your parents have photographs taken when they were young, and even if they have earlier pictures of the family. Remember that two or three generations of a family can extend well over a hundred years and think of the changes which will have taken place. You will be able to see what sort of clothes your great-grandparents wore, the toys they played with, their animals, and

Family photographs show the clothes our parents and grandparents used to wear

the rooms they lived in. Most early pictures were taken in photographic studios, and mounted on stiff cards, and you will find that the designs on the backs of the cards also make an attractive collection. Ask your parents or an old relation to name the people in the pictures as identities are quickly forgotten.

If you are lucky, you can find an album for your pictures so they are not damaged. Sometimes there are pretty double frames for them, or small pressed metal frames which were put on to the picture by the photographer. Early pictures were on fine metal instead of paper and were protected by thin tin frames and sometimes these are mixed up with old brooches and buttons in junk boxes.

Some interesting museums where you can see photographs are: The Kodak Museum, Wealdstone, Middlesex; The Science Museum, Exhibition Road, London sw7; The National Portrait Gallery (Photographic Collection), 15 Carlton House Terrace, London sw1.

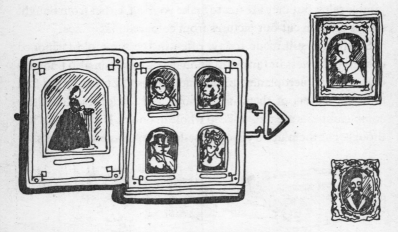

A family album keeps photographs safely, or they may be protected by attractive gilt frames

Scraps

Early scraps were printed sheets of brightly coloured pretty pictures which were cut with fine scissors and mounted on sheets of paper or in scrapbooks to make patterns. Sometimes they were printed as part of a wrapping for a product such as Colman's starch so that children could collect series of pictures for their albums.

Later, scraps were printed in sheets on thick shiny paper with embossed patterns, and these did not have to be cut out carefully but simply taken apart. They were often designs of pretty costumes, military uniforms, animals, or flowers, and as well as being put into books, they were often used to decorate greetings cards, or put on to boxes or screens. The boxes and screens were completely covered with glued-on scraps and then varnished to give a smooth, hard surface. Sometimes you can see old screens in auctions or jumble sales, but they are fun to make yourself, either from bought scraps or from cut-out pictures from coloured magazines.

Scraps are still made today, often in the same old-fashioned designs of flowers or farmyard animals, but you can also find new ones of cars, aeroplanes, trains and horses. You can often find quite old sheets of them in toyshops and stationers, and these complete sheets are nice to keep whole in books. If you have a lot, though, cut them up to cover loose-leaf files or exercise books, or

Scraps of motor transport, planes and ships are popular today

Sentimental cherubs are a favourite scrap design

Clasped hands are based on a Victorian design

Flowers are another popular scrap design

Scraps often show nursery rhyme characters, such as the little boy bringing a little nut tree

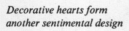

Decorative hearts form another sentimental design

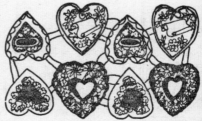

to decorate a wastepaper basket or lampshade. You can varnish them with thin clear varnish to make them really permanent and firm.

Newspaper cuttings

Most families have a newspaper every day, and some have two or three, and it is not difficult to make a collection of papers or cuttings. Really old papers of course can be very valuable, but everyday papers are just as much fun to read and keep. If you have space, whole newspapers can be collected, but they do take up a lot of room. This is worthwhile for special issues for coronations, royal weddings or funerals, or for events like the first moon landing, or for disasters or happenings which particularly interest you. You could just collect a whole newspaper each year on your birthday and see what has happened over quite a long period, and how fashions and ideas change. Keep the papers clean and uncrumpled and away from mice or insects.

Cuttings are easier to collect and can be made up into collages, scrap screens or book covers. If you want to use scrapbooks, make

Saturday October 18 1958

Disaster headline from a newspaper which is no longer in print

Terror came to a village

50

sure they are big, as photographs or cartoons should be kept whole, although the printed text can be cut if necessary. Mount the cuttings with the name of the paper and the date.

A lot of people have made interesting collections of news about the royal family through the years. Others collect all the information about their favourite sport, or cup finals, or certain crimes. You might collect information on space exploration, or on discoveries in science or archaeology, or on clever animals, or on the theatre or ballet. You might like to collect cartoons by your favourite artist, or about special subjects such as politics. If you like jokes, try collecting misprints, or only headlines containing your name or initials. Your name might be quite ordinary, but if it is the same as someone who is often in the news, you will find a lot of funny headlines which apply to you as well.

DAILY EXPRESS
Friday August 9 1974

EXIT NIXON
Drama as U.S. waits to hear him say it

Instant history in a newspaper headline

Unintentional jokes often occur in headlines

Doctors beat Vicars
A doctors versus vicars charity cricket match on Sunday at

Evening Standard 4p

HOMAGE TO THE UNCROWNED KING

King Edward VIII Duke of Windsor. Born June 1894 Died May 1972

A good example of a story about a clever animal

Musician's cat warns of blaze
Evening Standard Reporter

The royal family is a popular subject for newspaper collectors

51

Comics

The first comic strip appeared in an English magazine in 1847, and the first comic paper in 1874. Nowadays, people enjoy collecting old comics, and a year or two ago there was even an exhibition of them in London. You probably already have quite a lot of your own saved up at home, and you'll find it interesting to ask your father what sort of comics he had and whether he has any old ones he has treasured.

Pip, Squeak and Wilfred were popular characters in a Daily Mirror *comic strip and in annuals in the 1920s and 1930s*

Superman, Billy Bunter and Mickey Mouse appeared regularly in favourite comics

Early comics were amusing, with *Comic Cuts* and *Chips* running from 1890 to 1953. Others like *Hotspur* and *Magnet* contained stories and serials which appealed to schoolboys in particular. *Puck* and *The Rainbow* were other favourites with small children, but gradually gave way to Mickey Mouse and his own comic which started in 1936. America introduced *Superman* and *Batman* at the end of the 1930s, while England was enjoying *Film Fun* and *Radio Fun* featuring favourite characters in amusing situations. In the 1940s, *Eagle, Girl* and *Robin* were introduced and they combined colourful strips with stories and general information. An early version of the educational magazine was *The Children's Newspaper*, and in the last few years there have been many children's magazines or comics which have been mainly educational.

Comic magazines have continued with *Cor, Whizzer & Chips, Beano* and *Dandy*, but there are now more papers featuring favourite pop stars. In the comic papers, the same characters go on appearing for years, but in pop papers, they change very quickly. If you collect them for a year or two, you will be surprised at the difference. Try to keep comics flat and clean, and arrange them in order of issue. At jumble sales you will often find bundles of comics which are fun to read, and can be quite valuable to keep. If you want to know more about comics, read *Discovering Comics* (published by Shire).

A huge range of weekly comics was available during the first fifty years of this century

Greetings cards

Since Victorian times, people have enjoyed sending each other birthday and Christmas cards, and special Valentine cards. If you like to keep your own special cards each year, you may find you already have quite a collection, and you might enjoy looking for early ones. See if your parents or other older members of the family have treasured their cards and will let you have them. They can be mounted in postcard albums, or in scrapbooks, or arranged and catalogued in shoe-boxes. Don't stick them down on paper, because if you start to get special ones you might want to swop them, or even sell them.

A few cards are very plain with only words of greeting on them, but most are either pretty or funny. People have particularly liked sending each other pictures of flowers or animals, and cards in Victorian and Edwardian days were often decorated with cut-out lace edges or pretty scraps. Many cards were elaborately folded or had cut-out designs, and children's cards were made like paper

*Flowers and horseshoes
for a birthday card*

*Victorian Christmas card with the
traditional robins and holly*

Amusing animals were favourites for Victorian Christmas cards

An elaborately gilded cut-paper Valentine card

toys. Children used to like particularly pictures of animals dressed up, and of funny policemen.

Valentine cards were very elaborate, with a lot of paper lace, silver paper and hand-painted designs. Often you can find them in their own pretty envelopes. This kind of elaborate design was also used for mourning cards which are not sent out now, but used to be given to close friends and family when people died. Some are just plain white cards with black edges, but others are elaborately printed in silver and purple, or have cut-out paper designs, and they have their own special envelopes too. You may find some in drawers or boxes at home, but they are quite often tucked into boxes of postcards in junkshops or bookshops.

Memorial card and envelope sent to friends and family after a death

Cigarette cards

Cigarette-card collecting is called cartophily, and is now very popular, although cigarette packets no longer contain cards. Cigarettes first became popular after the Crimean War and plain cardboard slips were used to stiffen flimsy packs. Later, these were printed with an advertisement of the name of the make, a description of the cigarettes and a copy of the packet design. About 1879, the Americans put pictures on the cards, and in 1885 W.D. & H.O. Wills were the first British tobacco company to put picture cards in their packets. Usually there were fifty cards in each set, but sometimes the sets consisted of as few as four or twelve cards.

A history lesson was provided by the series of kings and queens of England

 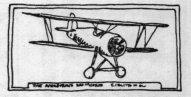

'New' forms of transport on cigarette cards

The pictures were of kings and queens of England, flowers, fishes and animals, film stars, military uniforms and transport. On the back of each card was a description and plenty of information on the subject. Special albums were provided in which cards could be stuck, and the information from the back of each card was also printed in the album. If you have loose cards, or bundles of them, keep them carefully and cleanly in boxes.

It is not easy to pick up cards in shops now because many people are collecting them, but you may find your parents or grandparents have a small collection from their childhood. You can buy cards through the London Cigarette Card Co. Ltd, 34 Wellesley Road, London w4, who produce catalogues and a magazine called *The Cigarette Card News*. You can also join the Cartophilic Society of Great Britain, Clewin, Maidenhead Road, Windsor, Berkshire.

Natural history was a lesson taught by the collecting of cards

Film stars were popular subjects for 1930s cigarette cards

Programmes and menus

If you go to a theatre, or a sports match or a concert, you will probably come away with a programme. Even if you don't go to such things yourself, older friends or family may. Some programmes are simply lists of scenes and names, or short descriptions of musical pieces, but others are full of photographs of the people taking part, or they may be elaborate souvenir programmes specially printed to commemorate an occasion. All kinds of programmes are fascinating records of what happened, and it can be fun to look back and see who used to be famous, or perhaps find only a small mention of somebody who later became very famous indeed.

If you enjoy sport, you can collect programmes from football and cricket matches, tennis tournaments, ice hockey, horse shows, and even the Olympic games. If you prefer other kinds of entertainment, there are theatre and circus programmes, music concert programmes and programmes for fêtes, pageants and galas. Perhaps your school makes its own programme each year for an open day or sports day and you will have quite a collection of these by the time you leave school. Your parents or grand-

Charity ball programme, sports programme and theatre programme

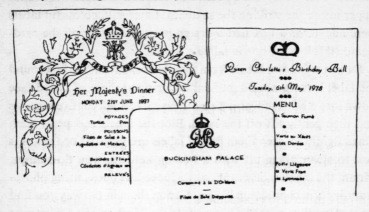

parents may have saved programmes of events they went to, or catalogues of special exhibitions they enjoyed. See if they have any of the souvenir programmes which commemorate royal occasions such as coronations, jubilees or silver weddings.

Souvenir menus can also be interesting to collect. You will have to ask for a menu from a restaurant or hotel if you have been given a meal for a special treat, but perhaps your family or friends will have some unusual menus for parties or dances they have been to, for special events, or even from ships they have travelled on where a new menu is printed for each meal.

Matchbox labels

Matchbox-label collecting is called phillumeny, and there are hundreds of thousands of labels to collect. In Sweden, there are more than 40,000 varieties, and in Japan more than 30,000, for instance. The first friction matches were invented in 1826 by John Walker of Stockton-on-Tees, and they were packed in tin containers. Later, they were packed in cardboard boxes with sandpaper inside for striking the matches. Later still, colourful labels were added, or a box had a design printed directly on the cardboard (this kind of box is called a 'skillet').

Do not try to tear labels from their boxes, but cut the box round the label leaving a wide margin, and put the piece of board face down into a bowl of warm water. Leave it to soak for five minutes and then gently lift off the label. Blot the labels and press them down lightly to keep them flat. If labels are very old or frail, it is best to steam them off with a boiling kettle as you do stamps. Mount the labels in a scrapbook or loose-leaf book, using photographic corners or stamp hinges. Group them in the way you find most attractive, according to country, subject or age. Sometimes the same design has been used for many years but with slight

A variety of matchbox labels including an early one from a station automatic machine, book matches, miniature boxes and decorative gift matches

variations, and it is interesting to collect the same design printed at different dates.

Among designs which have been used are traditional puppets in Java, theatrical characters and landscape paintings in Japan, regional costumes in France, playing cards and costumes in Sweden and sporting events in Czechoslovakia. India issues rather crude and colourful designs which are made in people's homes instead of factories. The Australians like famous sayings on their boxes, while the English used to enjoy unusual facts and funny jokes. Road safety slogans, war propaganda and farm safety hints have all been printed on boxes.

Book-match covers can also be collected, and have been produced by travel firms, restaurants, charities and individuals. If you like these, take out the matches, press the covers flat and slot them through slits in scrapbook pages. If you are really interested in matchbox and book-match cover collecting, you can join the British Matchbox Label & Booklet Society, 283-285 Worplesdon Road, Guildford, Surrey.

Postmarks

You probably look quite carefully at stamps on letters, but the postmarks can be just as interesting, and much cheaper to collect.

Foreign postmarks show a variety of styles

As early as the seventeenth century, people ran private delivery services and letters were marked to show the date on which they were sent, and later the place they were dispatched from. When stamps were first issued in 1840, postmasters marked the stamps with a special cross to prevent second usage, and these postmarks have been developed all over the world.

If you collect postmarks, be sure not to tear them off letters, but to keep the whole envelope. You will find there are special marks from the armed forces abroad, from the House of Commons and, of course, from different countries. You could just collect marks from your own country, or from seaside towns, or from foreign countries.

There are also Post Office marks used to indicate errors such as under-stamping and incorrect addressing, and the designs of these change from time to time and are worth collecting. Another kind of mark is put on to advertise towns, or their products, or to

Advertising marks and a variety of modern postmarks

Censorship mark from Germany

Elaborately designed postmarks from the early twentieth century

commemorate special anniversaries or events, but these are in addition to the usual cancellation mark. You could collect those which have sporting themes, or which advertise different industries.

There is a good book called *Collecting Postal History* (published by Lowe), and you can join the British Postmark Society, 42 Corrance Road, London sw 5.

Food and wine labels

Many foods and drinks have colourful and interesting labels, but the three main kinds which people collect are those from cheese, fruit and wine. There is nothing to stop you collecting sugar wrappers, canned-fruit labels, or food labels from one country only, but you will find it easier to swop information if you stick to the three main groups.

Fruit labels are usually thin tissue wrappers printed with coloured designs. Tomatoes and melons are sometimes wrapped, but orange wrappers are the ones most often seen. Oranges were first wrapped in Victorian times to protect them and to act as an advertisement for the grower. Early wrappers were very bright and gay, but today's are made of very thin tissue with less elaborate printing. They have depicted such things as sunbursts and rainbows, classical themes, animals or merchants' trade marks, and very often the designs are funny. More than fifty different countries have issued these wrappers, and the Victoria & Albert Museum in London has a splendid collection and has published a wall chart showing their designs. People who collect orange wrappers are called citro-tegumentalists.

The collecting of cheese labels is called fromology and one col-

Wrappers from lump sugar

Cheese labels are small and easy to mount in books

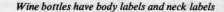
Wine bottles have body labels and neck labels

Jar labels often have old-fashioned designs

lector has more than 22,000 different labels. You can collect triangular labels, labels from half-boxes or complete boxes, labels from a particular country or a single manufacturer. There are 10,000 different labels in Switzerland alone, and they range from 12 mm (½ in) diameter to 600 mm (2 ft) square. If you want to know more about them, you can join the Fromologists' Circle, 18 Stonor Road, London W14.

Brightly coloured tissue wrappers from oranges and tomatoes

Wine bottles usually have two labels, one being large and square and the other being small and decorative, stuck higher up on the neck. You could collect both kinds, and could concentrate on labels from one country, or of one year, or of one type of wine.

You will have to soak off wine labels, but cheese labels are better without soaking and should be eased off the silver or waxed paper wrapping or box. Fruit labels are usually printed directly on the thin tissue wrappers and these wrappers should be kept intact. Fruit wrappers can be ironed and mounted on card or in a book. Wine and cheese labels can be put into a loose-leaf album or scrapbook, and should be mounted with stamp hinges in case you want to exchange them. Arrange labels in the way you want them classified and write down the name of the manufacturer, the country and the date. For protection, labels can be covered with a sheet of transparent paper.

Postcards

The first plain postcard was issued in Austria in 1869, and a year later, ready-stamped postcards could be bought and sent from British post offices for a total price of ½d (one old halfpenny). This was much cheaper than the penny post for a letter in an envelope, and half a million cards went through a London sorting office on the first day. Cards came into general use for people to write and receive answers quickly in the days before the telephone, but picture postcards did not come into general use until the end of the nineteenth century. Old cards are now becoming very valuable, and collectors are called deltiologists. Many families have a lot of cards tucked away in desks and drawers, and some can still be bought very cheaply.

The cards produced between 1894 and 1920 are widely collected now, but they were printed by the million, so you can still find plenty of them (usually you can tell the date from the postmark). Cards posted before 1910 or connected with a special event, such as the first British aerial post in 1911, are worth the most. There were funny postcards and pretty postcards, pictures of famous places and beautiful actresses, and of animals and sentimental scenes or stories. It is a good idea to specialize in one kind of card, perhaps of a place you know well, or of famous events, or posted before a certain date. Look for a postcard album to keep them in so that they can be slotted into place and the stamp, postmark and message will not be spoiled. The messages are great fun to read and can tell you a lot about the way of life years ago.

*Famous actresses and beauties were
favourite postcard subjects*

MISS GERTRUDE ELLIOTT

*Postcards slotted into old-fashioned albums can be removed so that the backs can
be read*

Jokes and puns were popular on holiday postcards

Another punning postcard from a fishing port

Postcards were often made from news pictures of accidents or unusual events

Some postcards were printed and produced very quickly. When family photographs were taken, either in a studio or at the seaside, they could be made into postcards, and you may find some of your own grandparents or great-grandparents. Postcards of disasters were also popular. If there was a train or bus crash, or a big fire, the local newspaperman used to take a picture, and postcards of the accident could be sent within a few hours of its happening. Sometimes there would be a second picture taken a day or two later when the debris was being cleared away.

It doesn't matter if you can't find any really old postcards. You can still find funny postcards of places and people, and there are also many pictures of animals, famous houses, railway engines, museum exhibits and almost everything else you might be interested in.

Rubbings

There are some things which you cannot actually collect, but you can record them, and make a collection of the records. Instead of drawing or photographing them, you can make rubbings on paper, which are great fun to do. Many people know about rubbing brasses on the floors or walls of churches, but you can also make rubbings of gravestones, coal-holes, tree barks and coins. Anything which has a texture or a pattern which stands up from a surface can be rubbed, such as the edge of a plate or even a dried grass or piece of netting or lace. Start with one or two small things like church brasses or coal-holes. Coal-holes can only be seen in

Everyday coins make interesting rubbings

Coal-hole patterns in towns are very varied and some people specialize in rubbing them

HERE LIETH
The body
of
JOHN REES
Who Departed this Life
Oct\\r the 17\\th 1824

Gravestones yield unusual rubbings

Brass to commemorate an infant who died at birth, wrapped in swaddling clothes

HERE SLEEP A NOBLE PAIR
WHO WERE IN LIFE
HE BEST OF HUSBANDS
SHE OF WIVES THE WIFE

May 18
1660

John and Susanna
Bissell

Another unusual gravestone for rubbing. Other designs often show a person's occupation by symbols such as farmworker's tools or sailing gear

71

city streets where they were used for delivering coal to cellars under the road. Coal-holes were called 'opercula' by Dr Shepherd Taylor who published a book about them after he had started to make rubbings in 1860 when he was a medical student.

If you want to rub a brass in church, you must get the permission of the vicar. You may have to write to him, or there may be a notice in the church to tell you where to apply, with a box for some money, and it is only fair to pay something for permission to rub a brass. Some brasses are tiny, but others can be life-size, and the rubbings can be mounted to hang on a wall. Dust the brass lightly before you start and stick down a sheet of thin paper with a few

Brasses of a knight who died in battle, and of a lady with her pet dog

pieces of tape. Kneel by the side of the brass and feel the edge carefully with your fingers so that you get the outline. Rub gently, to and fro, from side to side with a piece of heelball which is hard black wax from the shoemender or an artists' supply shop. Don't rub over the outline of the brass, and when you have completely finished, give the rubbing a smooth effect by going over the blackened part with a soft cloth.

You can learn all about armour and medieval clothes from these brasses. Many are of soldiers and their wives, but some are of clergymen, and even of skeletons, and in one Norfolk church there is a group of choirboys. If a soldier has his feet on a lion, it means that he died in battle, but if his feet are on a dog, he returned to hunt his hounds. You can get all the paper and other materials you need from an artists' supply shop, but start simply at first. Later on, you can use coloured papers and wax if you like. Be sure to record where the brasses or gravestones are and the date on which you rubbed them. Two good books which will help you to rub properly, and also tell you where to find unusual brasses, are: *Brasses & Brass Rubbings* (published by Blandford Press) and Macklin's *Monumental Brasses* (published by Allen & Unwin).

Manufactured objects

Advertising materials

In the middle of the last century, manufacturers began to package their goods and sell them all over the country instead of just in their local towns and villages. They began to advertise and to make packets distinctive so that they could be recognized everywhere, and they used many well-known artists for their designs.

Metal posters were popular for advertising. They were attached to the shops which sold the goods, and also to prominent walls, and men were specially employed to find good sites. These signs are not used for advertising now, but there are many old ones still on walls. If you want to collect them, they can be found in a lot of shop and garage yards, or in gardens, being used as part of sheds or fences. They are rather large to display and really need to be nailed up on a wall or in a shed or garage. Paper posters which are

Mugs and a glass for favourite drinks

74

*Bottle opener, pencil and spoon
given away by manufacturers*

really old are not easy to find as they were easily destroyed, but many modern copies can be found, as well as posters for today's goods. The older ones are very amusing as jokes were often used to announce exhibitions, plays and circuses, and these make a good collection on their own.

*Ashtray and beer mats
advertising a variety of brews*

Many firms think that it is a good idea to make everyday objects into advertisements, so that people see them constantly and remember names or products. Nowadays you can find beer mats, trays, pens and pencils, book matches, badges and drinking glasses. A few years ago, there was more money to spend on this kind of advertising, and there were many miniatures made of food containers, such as tiny biscuit tins and bottles, as well as mugs for special drinks, key rings, printed mirrors, pencil sharpeners, rulers, tape measures, magnifying glasses and even snuff boxes.

You may like to collect advertising material for only one product or firm, or you could collect only mugs or beer mats for instance. There are probably one or two pieces of advertising material already in your house, or you will find things on market stalls. A letter to your favourite firm sometimes produces a small

String puzzle advertising Michelin tyres in France

PVC aprons with designs from famous packages are a form of advertising

collection of posters, booklets and miniature items, or they may be offered as consolation prizes in competitions, or as special offers in exchange for tokens or labels.

Tins and boxes

The first biscuit tins were made for the customers of Huntley & Palmer's little biscuit shop at Reading, where stage-coach travellers stopped to get food for the journey ahead. Thomas Huntley's brother was an ironmonger and made tins to keep the biscuits fresh, but by 1870 the tins were made by machine and came in all sorts of fancy shapes. In 1970, the Victoria & Albert Museum had an exhibition of biscuit tins, taken from a private collection of over 6000. Many were in the shape of books, birds' nests, clocks, houses, fishing baskets and bags of golf clubs. Before 1860, the original tins were completely plain, with paper labels. A few years later, tins were decorated with colour transfers, but in 1875, Barclay & Fry started printing directly on tin, so that the designs were not so easily scratched. Later tins were shaped and embossed after printing. If you want to collect biscuit tins, try concentrating on a special group, perhaps with royal family pictures, or country scenes, or tins designed for the nursery. Decorative tins were also made for tea, and even for presentation packs of mustard and other spices, and for sweets.

Baking powder, treacle and sweet tins, still made today in original designs

Painted wooden boxes from Oxfam

French soap box

Box for face powder and pill box

Cigarette packets for favourite old brands

All kinds of tins for food or household cleaning materials can be interesting. Look particularly for tins which held cocoa, treacle, baking powder, beef cubes and spices. Special tins containing a present of chocolate or sweets from the royal family were sometimes issued to the army. Look out too for old tobacco and cigarette tins and boxes, and containers for cleaning materials and laundry starches or soaps.

If you don't like the idea of food tins and boxes, there are many

Tin for saddle soap

Old biscuit tin made to look like a shelf of books

Painted metal tea tin of the type formerly used by grocers, and painted wooden tea box from Russia

Tiny tin used for gramophone needles

other attractive boxes which were used for all sorts of storage. Try looking for stamp boxes, or those for pills, cosmetics, studs, string, rings and other jewellery. You can find them made in unusual woods, or with painted designs, or they may be made in leather or metals, or decorated with shells, straw patterns or seeds. A lot of different boxes turn up at home anyway, but there are always plenty at jumble sales and in junk shops, and some very nice ones can sometimes be found at charity shops.

Dolls and soft toys

People have always loved dolls and for centuries children have cuddled them. Some early dolls are very simple, consisting of carved wood, or little sausage shapes of leather or cloth, but today there are hundreds of different kinds from every country in the world. Dolls have been made of china and wax, knitted fabric, string, clothes-pegs, moss, shells, spoons and plastic materials.

Early dolls are very rare and expensive, although you may find your mother or grandmother still has some interesting ones. There were delicate dolls made of wax, sometimes with cloth bodies, and others made of fine china. Early wooden dolls were jointed, and some china ones had movable limbs. If you find these in their original costumes, they are very special indeed.

Today's dolls are not so pretty, but they usually have a huge range of clothes which can make a good collection. You may already have an Action Man, Cindy, Barby or Mary Quant doll,

Painted wooden nesting dolls from Russia

Primitive doll, and dolls made from string and wool

American Kewpie doll which was very popular in the early twentieth century

Historical costume doll

but it is also fun to find other modern dolls with unusual costumes. There are sets of dolls made to look like historical characters, or like the old traders of London, or nursery-rhyme characters, and you can also find dolls dressed in regional costumes. There are Welsh, Scottish and Irish dolls, Cornish and Breton fishermen, Dutch dolls and other costume dolls from all over the world.

Some of these are very strange indeed. In Denmark, there are knitted dolls which make egg cosies. Russia has pilgrim dolls and wooden nesting dolls. In Norway, reindeer moss dolls bring good luck to the forest workers, while male dolls have a leather patch on the back of their trousers. The size of the patch on a man's trousers

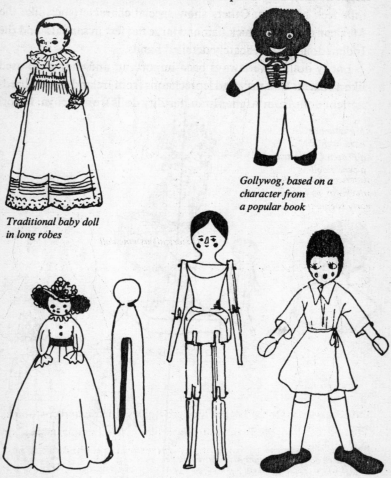

Traditional baby doll in long robes

Gollywog, based on a character from a popular book

Wooden doll made from a clothes-peg, a jointed wooden Dutch doll and a modern Austrian wooden doll

indicates how rich he is – the bigger the better. In Portugal, they are very fond of special dolls. There are fishergirls with the traditional nine petticoats, bridal dolls, and worker dolls such as bull-tenders and washer-women. Sometimes, dolls show the products of their regions, such as Welsh dolls with their flannel clothes and their little leek brooches. Others show special characteristics, like the Mexican dolls with thick hair and large flat feet in sandals, and the Indian dolls with delicately detailed hands.

Lucky dolls have always been important, and they were used like a charm. You may find leprechauns from Ireland, lucky dried-apricot dolls from Afghanistan, fertility dolls from Kenya, Maori

Miniature doll's head in china, a Frozen Charlotte and a pedlar doll

Modern dolls, like Action Man, have a huge wardrobe of clothes which can be changed and added to

84

dolls with a lucky charm or tiki around their necks. Today's lucky dolls include the pixies and skeletons people hang in their cars, the trolls of Scandinavia and corn dollies made for harvest.

A lot of people buy dolls as souvenirs, and once people know that you collect them they will perhaps bring them for you. One new kind of souvenir is the rag doll printed on a cut-out sheet, which is sold by the National Trust and Oxfam among other charities, and which you can make up yourself. If you like odd kinds of dolls, you might like to collect small finger puppets, Chinese twin

Welsh doll in traditional flannel, wearing a leek, with a Portuguese student doll and a French regional doll

Greek wedding dolls in elaborate costumes

Hungarian doll in elaborately embroidered costume

Native dolls dressed as an Eskimo, West Indian woman and Pakistani man

Traditional rag dolls, and cut-out Thai costume doll from Oxfam

doll rubbers and pencil ends, pipe-cleaner dolls, tiny felt model dolls and tumbler dolls. Other amusing oddments are china doll heads which used to be used for cakes and tea-cosies, china babies, and Frozen Charlottes which are tiny china dolls without movable limbs which were supposedly named after a little girl who drowned.

If you are very fond of your collection of dolls, you may like to arrange them in a glass-fronted cupboard. Some furniture for them could also be a part of your collection. Furniture has been made of cane, wood and even seeds strung together. Some pieces are very expensive as they were really test-pieces made by apprentice furniture-makers, but you can often find less special beds, tables and chairs in junk shops or at jumble sales.

You may prefer soft-toy animals to dolls (see Model animals), but there is one special character who is more like a doll than a soft toy. The Gollywog was a character in a book by Florence Upton and he became a popular nursery character with his smart trousers, waistcoat and jacket. You don't see many gollywogs around now, but they are worth looking for as they are real characters.

Dolls' furniture made in coloured cane

Victorian doll in elaborate costume

There are some good collections of dolls in many museums such as: The Bethnal Green Museum, Cambridge Heath Road, London E2; The Doll Museum, Oken's House, Castle Street, Warwick; Museum of Childhood, 38 High Street, Edinburgh; and Museum of Childhood, Water Street, Menai Bridge, Anglesey.

Trinkets

All kinds of small personal trinkets can be collected. These are the little pieces of decoration which people have used for centuries to make themselves and their clothes more attractive. When you have found a few bits and pieces, you will probably want to collect only one kind of trinket. Some of the things to start with might be buttons, buckles, beads, pieces of jewellery, hatpins and tie-pins,

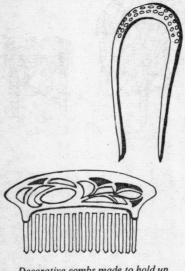

Decorative combs made to hold up ladies' long hair

Hatpins and tie-pins are safely kept in a large pincushion

Cufflinks and studs

Decorative cross, enamelled locket, china and metal brooches and a variety of charms

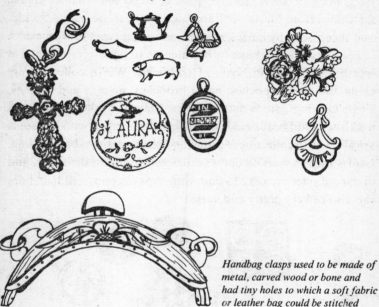

Handbag clasps used to be made of metal, carved wood or bone and had tiny holes to which a soft fabric or leather bag could be stitched

hair ornaments and make-up equipment like powder compacts and lipstick cases.

Many mothers keep a button box and you may find odd ones among them. There are buttons in glass, horn, metal of all kinds, wood, leather, fabric, mother-of-pearl, ivory, jet and plastic. Buttons with shanks, not with holes in them, are the most interesting to collect, except, that is, for pearl or linen buttons with holes. Sometimes you can find old cards of these in drapers' shops. You may like to collect buttons from military uniforms or from those worn by athletic clubs, private companies and banks, hotels and clubs, hunts, and some trades and professions. Otherwise, try collecting buttons in one kind of material, or with one type of pattern (such as flowers or animals).

Buckles come in all shapes and sizes. Look out for shoe buckles as well as belt buckles, and see if you can find buckles made in cut steel, brass or silver, leather, plastic, wood and enamel. Snake fastenings from fabric belts are interesting, as are badge buckles and those worn by nurses, soldiers and other types of workers.

Jewellery doesn't have to be valuable to be interesting, and is worth looking for in boxes of oddments. Worth collecting are china and shell brooches, name brooches, tie-pins and hatpins, single ear-rings, studs and cufflinks, charms, broken chains and necklaces. Odd beads made of amber, glass, paper, wood or seeds are also worth collecting together and can sometimes be re-strung. Ladies used to wear elaborate slides and combs in their hair, and discarded ones are easy to find; ring-clips for pony-tail hairstyles can also be very pretty and varied.

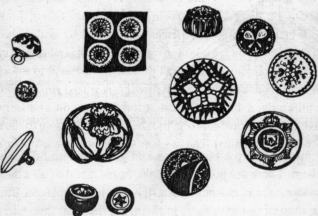

Buttons can be made of almost every material and can sometimes be found stitched to an original card for selling

Shoe and belt buckles in metal. The shoe buckles are small and have no prongs as they were sewn on to the shoes

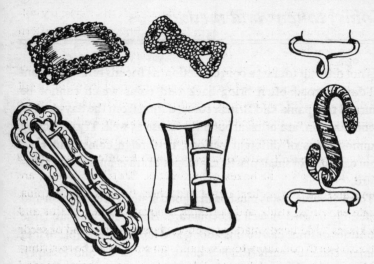

All kinds of trinkets can be arranged in boxes on a backing of soft paper, velvet or cotton wool. Small pieces like buttons and buckles are worth sewing on to cards. Hatpins, tie-pins and brooches can be displayed on large pin-cushions. Often, junk shops have little dressing-table trays made of china with small branched stands for rings, and these trays and ring-stands are very attractive for displaying jewellery. Trinkets can be seen in many museums, and there are many specialist shops where you can see and buy all kinds of buttons. Most stores in London and large towns have good button departments, and it is worth going to look at a specialist shop called The Button Queen, St Christopher's Place, London WI.

Coins, tokens and medals

It is not difficult to start a coin collection, as friends returning from holidays abroad often bring back odd coins which cannot be returned to a bank. Old British coins, dating from the days before decimalization, are often around the house as well. Try collecting common coins of different periods, or foreign coins, and keep them carefully in small plastic envelopes or trays made from cardboard.

To be of value, coins must be in a good state of preservation and preferably unused as well as being rare. However, there are large quantities of some early coins about, and it may be possible to find Roman coins or early English coins quite easily and cheaply. Never clean coins with abrasives or try to polish them. A little warm soapy water removes grease from gold and silver.

If you like coins, you may also be interested in collecting medieval jettons which were counters used to help add up accounts. Tradesmen also used to issue tokens as a kind of private coinage for giving small change, and these have the name of the shop and the place on them. In the last century, tradesmen and

Two of the smallest British coins –
a silver threepence, and a farthing

Austro-Hungarian gold Corona in presentation box –
a traditional christening present

Foreign coins show a huge variety of designs

manufacturers gave decorative tokens to advertise themselves, and this was copied a few years ago by garages. You may already have some of these tokens which had pictures of footballers, cars and aeroplanes on them. French petrol stations gave away a collection of tokens commemorating Napoleon's life.

Medals are also very interesting to collect and you can find them for all sorts of occasions. Gallantry medals, such as the V.C. or G.C., are of course very rare and valuable, but thousands of medals were given to members of the armed forces who served in various campaigns. Medals are also issued to policemen for special duties, and to nurses who reach certain positions, or you may find

Threepenny piece, halfpenny and an old English penny

Traders' tokens and commemorative tokens issued by petrol companies

Historic car tokens collecting card issued by petrol company

Miniature medals, coronation medal and Portuguese presentation medal

old school medals, or those given away to commemorate coronations or the opening of famous buildings.

If you become very interested in your collection of coins, you may be able to join a local branch of the British Association of Numismatic Societies. There is also the Royal Numismatic Society and the British Numismatic Society. Particularly good collections of coins and tokens can be seen at: The Assay Office and City Museum, Newhall Street, Birmingham; The Fitzwilliam Museum, Trumpington Street, Cambridge; The British Museum, Great Russell Street, London WC1; and The Ashmolean Museum, Beaumont Street, Oxford.

Horse brasses

Before 1918, there were more than a million working farm-horses in Britain. This figure had dropped to 54,000 by 1960, and now few horses are used on farms. A few breweries still keep these big horses, as it is cheaper to use them for pulling heavy weights than to run large lorries.

The harnesses of farm-horses and horses used to pull carts were heavily decorated in shining brass ornaments. These brasses hung on leather straps and many of them were charms against evil. They were decorated with the signs of the sun, moon and stars, or with a bell to ring and frighten away evil spirits. Sometimes there were pictures of crops or ploughs, country animals or windmills or the crest of a landlord, or brasses commemorated great events such as coronations or famous victories. Railway horses had brasses with engine pictures, dockyard horses had ships or anchors, and brewers' horses had barrel emblems.

Modern brasses copy the old signs, but also portray famous

Small brasses for nailing to narrow harness straps

A variety of horse gear in use

people such as Churchill or Montgomery. Old brasses usually have rather rough backs showing the marks of the sand mould in which they were cast, and they often have small knobs on the back made by the melted metal as it was poured through a hole and later cooled back to its solid form. If you are lucky, you may find brasses fitted on to their original pieces of leather.

Other pieces of harness decoration may also be found. There were brass decorations attached to blinkers, buckles, and small brasses which were hammered on to narrow leather straps. These were usually about 35–50 mm (1½–2 in) wide, in simple shapes such as diamonds, circles or hearts. They had long prongs on the back which were hammered through leather and then flattened to secure the shapes. If you like digging around in fields and in old sheds,

96

Shoes vary from tiny racing plates to giant shoes for cart- and dray-horses

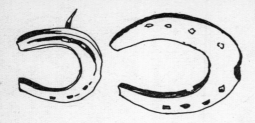

Plumed and crested terrets which were fixed to the top of the harness between the horse's ears

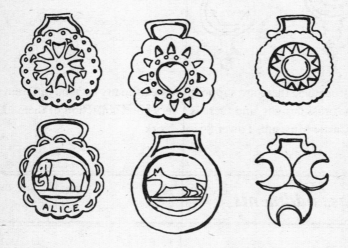

you may find pieces of bits, stirrups, spurs and horseshoes which can be added to your collection.

If you are very lucky, you may find another rather special kind of horse brass. This was the fly-terret, sometimes called a flyer or swinger, which was worn upright on the horse's head. This flyer is a circle with a swinging disc to catch the light, or sometimes a bell; often there was the addition of horsehair plumes coloured red, white and blue.

Traditional horse brasses which were strung on leather straps

Altogether, there are supposed to be as many as 3000 different horse brass designs, and there is a very good collection of them in the Castle Museum, Tower Street, York.

Glass oddments

It would be expensive to collect drinking glasses, decanters or paperweights, but there are thousands of small glass objects which were in everyday use and may now be tucked away in cupboards at home. A lot of them find their way to jumble sales or into junk shops, and it is easy to pick up things which are useful as well as pretty. Early glass was blown and many pieces were cut into elaborate designs. These can cost a lot of money, so the glass to look for is that which has been moulded and pressed. This kind of glass

Heavily patterned glass cream jug and mug

Decorative sweet dish

Glass plate commemorating the 1953 coronation

was first made to imitate cut glass (you will be able to see if it is moulded because many of the things have a moulding line down one side).

You might like to have a mixed collection at first, but gradually you will find that some things, like bowls, are made in hundreds of patterns, so you can specialize in just one kind of glass item. To start with, there are fruit, sugar and ice-cream dishes, jugs, salt cellars, cake stands, jelly moulds and lemon squeezers, and even marbles and fishing floats (big coloured glass balls).

Salt cellars may only cost a penny or two and come in many sizes. They were very popular in the nineteenth century, and were usually used in pairs. Little sugar bowls and cream jugs were sometimes made to match, or sometimes jugs were made in sets of different sizes. Sweet dishes in glass were often made to look like

Cut glass stoppers from decanters

Coloured glass fairy-light holder with wire for hanging on a tree

Glass salt cellars come in hundreds of patterns

Pair of glass stands for carving knife and fork

Pressed glass bowls for ice-cream

little baskets, sometimes with handles that look like twigs. Ice-creams, jellies and custards were served in little cups or stemmed glasses which often resemble wine glasses.

100

There are other small pieces of glass which are not easy to recognize, and are often very cheap for this reason. Carving knives and forks used to be rested on short, pretty little stands made of china, metal or glass. Look for pairs of these, and also for toddy stirrers which gentlemen used to stir their drinks. These are rather like thick teaspoons with a flat end instead of a bowl, and you can often find them in boxes of oddments because people don't know what they are. They also don't recognize Victorian fairy lights with which people used to decorate their houses and gardens for special occasions. These look like large paste jars with a pattern like a fir-cone and come in pretty colours. A wire used to be tied around the top, and a nightlight put inside to make a little lantern. All coloured glass is pretty, and you might like to collect only red glass (usually called 'cranberry'), or that which is coloured blue, green or an unusual greenish-yellow.

Although complete decanters can be very expensive, odd stoppers are often heaped into boxes and cost very little. These are often of cut glass and come in thousands of pretty patterns. They are nice and small to collect, and very easy to display on a table or shelf.

Large glass plate commemorating
Queen Victoria's golden jubilee in 1887

Simple glass jelly mould

101

Badges

Badges were originally used to identify their owners. They were pictures or symbols of the men who wore them, particularly knights who had to be easily seen in battle. Military badges are very interesting to collect, made of metal, or of metal wire and coloured threads. As well as those made for the armed forces, there are badges worn by nurses and other groups of workers such as railmen and firemen.

Groups of people such as schools, clubs and organizations like Guides and Scouts like to have their own identifying badge. There are badges to identify businessmen, such as those who belong to Rotary Clubs, and politicians, such as the old Primrose League badge for the Conservative club founded by Disraeli. Sports enthusiasts like to collect football or cricket club badges, and there are badges for railway modellers, pigeon fanciers or traction-engine enthusiasts.

There are souvenir badges too, from such places as London Airport, from cross-channel steamers, and from museums and

Enamel lapel badges from an airport and station

Club, proficiency and school badges may be in metal or cloth

Metal Girl Guide badge and cloth proficiency badges

Club or souvenir badges may be in plastic or in cloth

Voluntary service organizations and schools have distinctive enamel badges

famous houses. Cloth badges commemorate various countries, towns and counties. Sometimes firms find it worth-while to issue advertising badges at exhibitions, and charities give badges to their helpers.

Look for badges in cloth, plastic and metal (both pin-on and buttonhole badges are made in metal). Your family may have

Airline badge with owner's name

Souvenir badge from an aeroplane collection

Sew-on badges for anoraks and jeans

Counties, towns and countries have their own sew-on cloth badges

some from clubs or organizations they belonged to when they were children, or places they have visited. Cloth badges can be mounted on a board or in a book, but it is more fun to sew them on to an anorak or trousers, or round a cloth hat. Metal badges can be pinned on to clothes too, or displayed on a large soft-toy animal or a cushion.

You can often find odd badges among trinkets at jumble sales or in junk stalls. If you want to find shops which sell badges, look in the weekly magazine *Exchange & Mart* for names. A good book to read is *Discovering British Military Badges and Buttons* (published by Shire).

Model animals

Model animals have been made and collected for nearly 5000 years. The Egyptians made dogs, elephants, cows, mice, camels, crocodiles, tortoises and lions in clay and wood. Many of the clay animals were glazed and brightly coloured, and often decorated with spots. The Greeks and Romans also had clay and bronze models of their domestic animals, but the Chinese made theirs in porcelain and precious stones. In India, model wooden animals are given as toys at a wedding. There are the traditional wooden horses of Sweden and the carved wooden bears of Russia and

Straw horse, Chinese horse, Swedish wooden horse and Indian horse

Lead rabbits and hutch from a model farm

Painted wooden cow

Finger puppet, dressed mouse and clockwork mouse

China panda and cat, glass seal and china lion

This wooden leopard from India is only about 35 mm (1½ in) high

Switzerland. Birds are popular too, sometimes made as toys, like the pecking hens of Greece and Russia, or their owls with flapping wings. There are woollen chickens and ducks to hang on prams to amuse children, and all kinds of animal toys such as walking horses, pull-along dogs, clockwork frogs and ladybirds, pre-1939 celluloid and later plastic animals, and of course the lead animals used for farms (now also usually made in plastic). Sometimes souvenir model animals were made when animals were first brought back for zoos. Look out for early models of the panda, and the okapi which looked like half zebra and half antelope.

Some model animals can also be soft and cuddly and used

instead of dolls. The teddy bear has been popular since the early part of the twentieth century when the American president, Teddy Roosevelt, saved a baby bear from being shot on an expedition and toy bears were called after him. The first pandas were brought to zoos in the 1930s and soft-toy pandas have been made ever since. The koala bear is another favourite as a souvenir from Australia.

You can collect just one kind of animal or bird if you like. People collect horses, dogs, cats, owls, bears, mice, pigs, hedgehogs, chickens, pandas and elephants. If you prefer, you can collect animals made in one material, such as stone, china, glass, fur, metal, straw or wood. Some people just like to collect metal farm animals, or Noah's Ark animals, or soft-toy animals. You probably already have quite a collection without realizing it, but look out for new ones in souvenir shops, Oxfam shops, Indian and Chinese craft markets, and on junk stalls.

108

Moneyboxes

Money used to be saved in small earthenware bowls called 'pigs'. Later earthenware was used to make models of real pigs with slits in the top for money, and these piggy-banks had to be broken to get out the savings. In Victorian families, money was carefully saved, and poor country people were encouraged to work hard to have enough to buy a pig to fatten up and feed the household. A pig in the sty became a sign of a hardworking and careful family. Piggy-banks have also been made in carved wood, fine china and plastic, and nowadays they have a hole in the bottom so that money can be taken out without breaking the pig.

Simple, square wooden boxes were also used for saving money, and sometimes had pretty painted lids. Victorian children had wooden moneyboxes made in the shape of cottages, or houses were made in pottery decorated with china flowers, and with a slit in the lid. Another favourite was the toy pillar-box made in red and black tin, in which money was posted instead of letters. The king's or queen's initials tell you when a tin was made, either VR, GR or ER.

Red tin pillar-box designed as a moneybox

American frog moneybox

Sentry box biscuit tin designed to be used later for money

Popular cartoon character Snoopy lies on a kennel moneybox

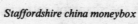

Staffordshire china moneybox

Cash boxes and bank boxes

110

Early Victorian wooden moneybox
house sold by a pedlar

Charity collecting box in a popular house shape

Two china piggy-banks and a Swedish wooden pig moneybox

The Americans called their moneyboxes 'banks' and liked making amusing ones. There were iron and tin houses made to look like real banks; a goat-butting bank, a fat man, a frog, a bear, and a man's head are other examples. Most of these banks had a mechanical action which was triggered off by putting money in. For instance, money was put on to the man's hand, and he lifted it to his mouth and nodded his head.

Today, charities like to collect money with working boxes.

When money is put in a box, you may find a lifeboat is launched, a dog goes down a slide, or a circus goes into action. Dr Barnardo's Homes follow the old tradition of using a model house to collect money.

Sometimes you will find little metal tubes for saving small coins. Before decimalization, these were used to collect sixpences. When £1 had been collected, the lid came off. Today, small coin-savers are used in cars for keeping money for parking meters.

Souvenirs

We all like to bring back things from our holidays to remind us of happy days, and these souvenirs can make an interesting collection, particularly if friends also bring you little gifts from holidays

Elaborately coloured and gilded china was a traditional present to bring back from holidays

Gay traditional patterns painted on household objects are typical souvenirs from the barges on canals

or business trips abroad. There are a lot of other kinds of souvenirs though.

Special things are always made for royal occasions such as coronations, jubilees and silver weddings. You can find mugs, glass plates, badges, flags, pottery figures and dishes, medals and coins, key-rings, spoons, horse brasses, sweet boxes and biscuit tins, scarves and handkerchiefs, stamps, pens and pencils, rosettes, and special magazines and newspapers. Most of these things were made for Princess Anne's wedding and Prince Charles's investiture. There have also been special souvenirs made to commemorate famous naval and military battles and large exhibitions, and many famous people who were honoured in their lifetime or on their death.

Alum Bay sand packed in coloured layers in glass from the Isle of Wight

113

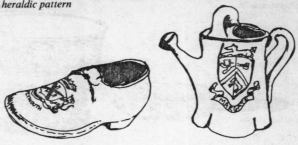

You may like to collect one kind of souvenir, such as handkerchiefs or mugs, or you may prefer a general collection of items commemorating one person, place or event. You could collect presents from the seaside, either from one place or from all those you have visited. Look out for the little china models with heraldic designs printed on them – the most expensive and fashionable ones were made by W. H. Goss, but there are plenty from other makers too. You could also try collecting all the items connected with one event, such as the first moon landing, or even Christmas plates and mugs.

If you are particularly interested in a person in history, you could find lots of things connected with him. Nelson and Shakespeare, for instance, have been commemorated with all kinds of china and glass, busts and pictures, postcards and models, and you may find copies of letters or documents about the person you are interested in.

Of course, some souvenir items can be very expensive, but you will probably find your family already has quite a few things bought when the items were newly made and cheaper, or given to them when they were children. People often get tired of their old souvenirs, and you can find them at jumble sales or on junk stalls. If you visit houses or museums, you can usually buy small souvenirs from their special shops.

Puzzles

Everybody loves puzzles. Long ago, a great maze was made in Crete, and today in England we can still see historic mazes at Hampton Court, Hatfield House and Winchester. These mazes were large puzzles made of paths edged by bushes or walls, along which people wandered until they could find an exit.

The Chinese were the first to invent a puzzle which they could solve indoors; it was called a Tangram. This kind of puzzle is a set of seven shapes cut in card or board which can be fitted together to form a square. This type of shape-fitting led to the fitting together of pieces to form a picture. These were used to educate children, and the first pictures were maps or illustrated natural-history lessons. These are known as jigsaws, because a 'jig' was the kind of saw used to cut the pattern. Old jigsaws are packed in wooden boxes with sliding lids, but the more modern ones come in cardboard boxes. There are so many kinds now that it is a good idea to collect only similar pictures, such as scenes from films, or places you have been to, or transport pictures, or famous paintings.

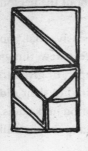

Tangram puzzle of seven pieces which can be made to form a square

Number puzzle with sliding numbers in a shallow tray

Pear-shaped three-dimensional wooden puzzle

Interlocking metal Chinese puzzles

Jigsaw puzzles were a popular form of educational toy

Another kind of picture puzzle is made with building blocks. As each block has six sides, it means that it is possible to make six different pictures from the same blocks. As these are really for small children, the pictures are usually of farmyards or simple nursery scenes.

More complicated puzzles are made in three dimensions. These are made as cubes or spheres of interlocking wood which break down into many pieces and are rather difficult to fit together. Usually they are made of plain polished wood, but sometimes they are coloured and can be in the shape of fruit or eggs.

In 1889, a man called Charles M. Crandell invented a puzzle which was a round tray about 150 mm (6 in) wide in which a marble had to be rolled until it fell into a hole. This was called 'Pigs in Clover' and sold very well, and developed into many small hand puzzles in which one or two balls had to be rolled along special routes or into holes. Often the puzzle is a brightly coloured picture, such as the face of a clown who catches the balls in his mouth or his eyes.

117

Other small hand puzzles are frames containing nine or sixteen movable squares which have letters, numbers or parts of a picture. The pieces have to be moved around to form words, number totals, or a complete picture. If you like intricate puzzles, you might look for small Chinese puzzles made of entangled metal which can be split into two pieces, or for puzzle rings which are made of a lot of tiny rings which have to be put together to form one finger ring.

Sewing things

Most families keep a sewing box, drawer or bag, full of all sorts of oddments for making and mending clothes. These boxes are often thrown away or sold to a junkman when a house is cleared out, and it is easy to find very old cotton reels, needle-cases, pincushions and such like. If you are very lucky, you may find an old box with special compartments for all these sewing accessories. You can specialize in one kind of needlework item, or start by finding examples of a lot of things, and perhaps work out when they were designed and used. Some are very ordinary, but others were meant as pretty souvenirs and little family gifts.

Cotton reels, for instance, may seem very ordinary, but they have changed a lot in the last hundred years. Elegant Victorian needlework boxes were fitted with spools of metal, bone or wood, often with decorative mother-of-pearl tops, for fine cottons.

Card bookmark with woollen or silk embroidered centre

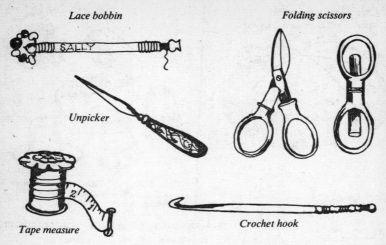

Lace bobbin

Folding scissors

Unpicker

Tape measure

Crochet hook

Embroidery silks were kept on cross-shapes of pearl or bone. Spare thread holders were often cut out of pretty cardboard and had decorative rounded ends so that the cotton or silk could not slip off. In the early twentieth century, wooden reels of cotton were sold, and in 1968, the first plastic cotton reels were introduced. Now these reels are giving way to long thin spools. Take particular notice of the colour of early threads—they are very clear and bright and quite unlike the colours we use today.

Some sewing things can be very rare and expensive, like

Large pincushion with embroidered bead pattern, and flat felt and embroidery hanging pincushion

119

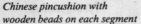
Chinese pincushion with wooden beads on each segment

Thimbles, including a Victorian gift thimble in a case and a silver Welsh hat thimble

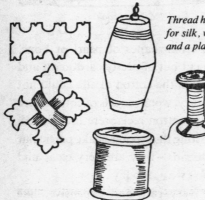
Thread holders, including mother-of-pearl holders for silk, wooden and card cotton holders, and a plastic cotton reel

thimbles. Even so, you may find little silver and brass ones with pretty patterns, sometimes even in their own cases. You may find small fine embroidery scissors, and neat little folding ones. There are souvenir needle-cases, either like little books or narrow tubes; some are hand-made in velvet or felt. Pincushions may be made to look like fruit or fat cushions, or they can be little pads of velvet set into the backs of metal or wooden animals. Giant pincushions in velvet embroidered with beads, or with a decoration of small silk flags were often made by sailors for their families or girl friends. Other things worth looking out for are tape measures, lace bob-

Needle holders made in wood, silver and cardboard

bins, tatting shuttles, crochet hooks, knitting needles, and the small penknives, unpickers and propelling pencils which were fitted into sewing boxes.

If you like to collect things made of paper, look out for perforated cards with printed patterns which were embroidered as bookmarks. Old paper patterns and fashion plates will show you the sort of clothes which used to be made at home or by a dressmaker using the sewing equipment you are collecting.

Old games

Old card and board games, marbles, dice and counters are great fun to collect because they can also be used by the family. You will probably find that you already have quite a collection, but you can often find old discarded games at jumble sales or on junk stalls. Although you may already have a game like Monopoly or Buccaneer, you may find an older one which has pieces made of metal and wood, which are much more interesting than today's plastic versions. If you go abroad on holiday, or have a friend who does, look out for foreign games, such as the many French editions of Happy Families.

Decorative marbles in clay and glass

A variety of dice including a teetotum which was spun like a top

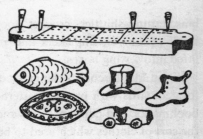
Games counters and a cribbage board for counting a score

Escalado, an early racing game

Many board games are very old, such as Ludo, Snakes and Ladders, Halma, Backgammon, Fox and Goose, Nine Men's Morris, and Solitaire, and the original boards were made of wood, ivory or ebony, often with brass trimmings. Later the games were sold more widely, and lighter boards were covered with cloth, and counters made of plastic. Some games were meant to teach children, and you may find geography and history games, or games of war strategy; others imitated adult pastimes, and there are many racing games, or such things as table croquet, table tennis and table football. Other popular games which had their own equipment were Spillikins, Dominoes, Tiddley Winks and Jacks; these are still played today, but the sets made even ten years ago look different from today's new ones.

122

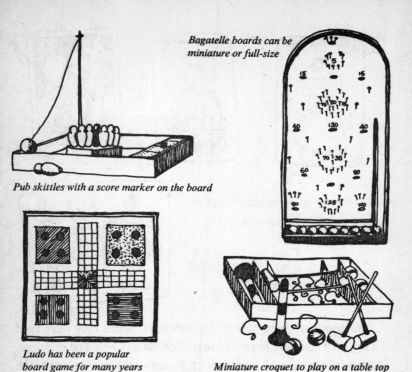

Bagatelle boards can be miniature or full-size

Pub skittles with a score marker on the board

Ludo has been a popular board game for many years

Miniature croquet to play on a table top

If you cannot find whole games, you may find all sorts of different counters. These have been made in bone, pottery, shell, metal and wood. Particularly attractive are mother-of-pearl and wooden fish which were used a lot by the Victorians. Dice are interesting too, made in bone, terracotta, wood or ivory. They were invented in Greece in 1400 B.C. and have been used ever since, sometimes with letters or figures instead of the usual spots. Look out for teetotum dice which used to be spun like a top.

Playing-cards are not difficult to collect as there are many modern ones made for advertising purposes. Sometimes you can find older packs in leather cases. If you enjoy playing unusual card games, look for old packs of Happy Families, Lexicon, Old Maid, Peter Rabbit, Bob's Your Uncle, Pit, and Panko (which commemorated the struggle for votes for women).

Old card games are fun to collect and play

Marbles have been played since 4000 B.C. when they were used in Egypt. They were popular too in the East, in Crete and in Rome, and were the special treasures of Roman soldiers. In 1788, the Hoffman marble-making machine was patented in England to make stone and wood marbles, but marbles have also been made in glass and clay. Variegated clay marbles are known as 'Dutch'; pink marbles with dark red veins in are called 'blood alleys'. The largest choice marbles are known as 'taws' or 'glassies', or in east London they are called 'glannies'.

There are old games in many museums. Some of the best are at: The Toy Museum, The Grange, Rottingdean, Brighton, Sussex; The Bethnal Green Museum, Cambridge Heath Road, London E2; The Museum of London, London Wall, EC2; Museum of Childhood, 38 High Street, Edinburgh; Pollock's Toy Museum, Scala Street, London W1 (also a shop); The Cornish Museum, East Looe, Cornwall; and Museum of Childhood, Water Street, Menai Bridge, Anglesey.

Dolls' houses, furniture and food

The first model rooms were made by the Greeks and Romans. They were three-sided rooms made of clay, with clay furniture. The first dolls' house was made for the daughter of the Duke of Saxony in 1558, and a few years later model houses with miniature furniture were popular in the Netherlands. These were not exact models of houses, but were like divided cupboards displaying tiny household objects, with the cupboard front looking like a real house. These first houses were not playthings, but were used by rich ladies to show small everyday items, often made in gold or silver, and given to them as little gifts.

In 1716, the first English model houses were called 'baby houses' as dolls were usually called 'babies' then. They were still only for

China tea service on matching tray

Silk carpet of the type given away in cigarette packets fifty years ago

Doll's food made from plaster, and straw vegetable basket

Set of cleaning implements for the dolls' house

rich families, and children were not really allowed to play with them. As well as complete houses, single open rooms were made and furnished as drawing rooms or kitchens, and children were allowed to play with open butchers' shops, drapers' shops, inns, market stalls and toy shops. Queen Victoria and Queen Mary both had dolls' houses complete with families of tiny dolls. The grandest dolls' house was ordered by Sir Neville Wilkinson in 1907 for his daughter, but it was not finished until she was grown up. It was sold in 1967 for £31,500 and was called Titania's Palace.

The completely furnished Nuremberg kitchen was an early form of dolls' house

Early furnishings were made of metal or wood, but there is also dolls' house furniture made of papier-mâché, plastic, matchboxes and horse chestnuts. You might like to collect only furniture, or perhaps you prefer kitchen equipment or tableware. There are sets of glasses and jugs, tea sets, pewterware from Germany, and brass cooking pots from India. Look out too for other things you like to see in a house, such as telephones, rows of miniature books, pots of flowers, dogs or cats in baskets, and garden tools and plants. Little silk carpets for dolls' houses used to be given away in cigarette packets and can often be found in junk shops.

If you like food, there is a whole menu to collect for the dolls' table. There are vegetables, hams, Christmas puddings, bowls of fruit, ice-cream, cakes, bacon and eggs. If you like to see people

Furniture made from horse chestnuts, pins and wool

Miniature maid to look after the furniture

127

Bedroom furniture made in wood and plastic

living in the dolls' house, look out for family dolls and the servants who used to wait on them. Tiny dolls made in china, wood, fabric, pipe cleaners or knitting include fathers, mothers, children, babies, maids, butlers and children's nurses.

There are dolls' houses and miniature furniture to be seen in many museums as well as in old houses which you can visit. Some of the most interesting are at: The Bethnal Green Museum, Cambridge Heath Road, London, E2; Audley End House, Saffron Walden, Essex; Windsor Castle, Berkshire (Queen Mary's Dolls' House); The Museum of London, London Wall, EC2; and The Rotunda, 44 Iffley Turn, Oxford.

Transport souvenirs

All sorts of things connected with travel can be collected, particularly things to do with trains and buses. It is probably easiest to start by collecting tickets, maps and timetables. These can be from lines which no longer exist, from regular journeys, from abroad, or from some of the small railway lines which are being reopened by enthusiasts. As well as regular travel tickets, there are also tickets for animals, excursions, workmen, the armed forces, bicycles and prams.

Bus, tram and train tickets, including commemorative tickets and those from private railway companies

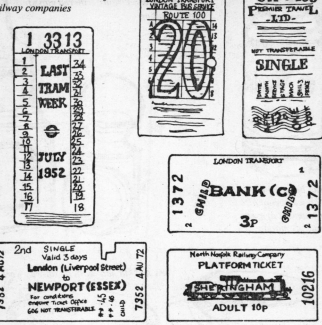

Wooden rack formerly used for holding tickets by the conductors of buses, trams and trolley-buses

If you have more space, you can collect the racks from which tickets were sold on buses, posters, uniform buttons and badges, whistles, railway signs, workmen's notebooks and caps, types of lamps or other small pieces of equipment which were used on old-fashioned stations. Of course, there are also photographs, postcards and books and magazines about transport.

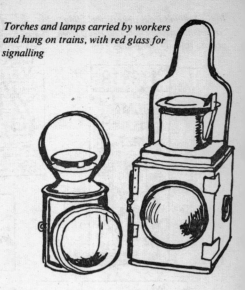

Torches and lamps carried by workers and hung on trains, with red glass for signalling

Ink bottle which formed part of office equipment at every railway station

New and old hats worn by railway workers

All collections are more fun if you find the things in odd places, or only pay a little for them, but if you are really keen you can buy things through advertisements in specialized magazines. There are also two Collectors' Corners (at Euston Station in London, and in Glasgow) where you can buy every kind of transport souvenir, right up to train nameplates which are very expensive.

There are many transport societies all over the country, some of which are run to provide funds for independent railways, but you can also join the British Young Travellers' Society, 41 Forest Hill Way, Dibden Purlieu, Southampton, Hampshire. If you are particularly interested in collecting tickets, you can join the Transport

Ticket Society, 18 Villa Road, Luton, Bedfordshire, which is a collectors' club and has a regular newsletter. Among museums with special collections are: Great Western Railway Museum, Faringdon Road, Swindon, Wiltshire; The Museum of Carriages, Mill Street, Maidstone, Kent; The Science Museum, Exhibition Road, London SW7; The Railway Museum, Stoneygate, Leicester; The Transport Museum, High Street, Hull; The Cheddar Motor & Transport Museum, Somerset; The Museum of Transport, Albert Drive, Glasgow; Transport Museum, Witham Street, Belfast, N. Ireland; and National Railway Museum, Leeman Road, York.

Toys

You probably take your toys for granted, although you may find you are already collecting some kinds, like railways or models or building toys. The same kinds of toys have been played with for centuries but their designs and materials change, and you may find it very interesting to collect old versions of the things you are still using today. Ask your family if they have any of their old toys and you will find them very different from the ones you are using. Visit almost any museum and you will find a collection of playthings.

131

Models of all types of vehicles and army equipment were made in lead but are now in lighter metals

Yo-yos are made in many different materials and sizes

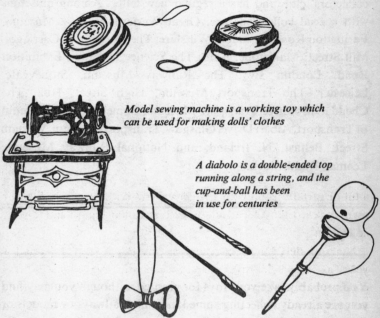

Model sewing machine is a working toy which can be used for making dolls' clothes

A diabolo is a double-ended top running along a string, and the cup-and-ball has been in use for centuries

If you like construction sets, look for Meccano and Lego, and for variations of these. For model-makers, there are planes, ships, cars, and even famous people to collect. Railways give tremendous scope for a collection. Apart from the track you use today, look for old engines, carriages and trucks, and for the stations and models which go with them. If you or your family go abroad, you will find

Trains and railway accessories make an interesting collection

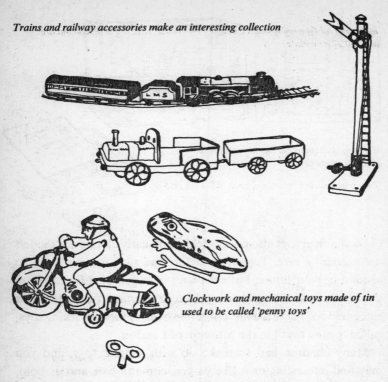

Clockwork and mechanical toys made of tin used to be called 'penny toys'

a lot of variations on your British system, but often these fit your own track so that you can add French or Italian equipment to your collection.

Scale models for dressing up railways have been popular for years, and so have farm animals, vehicles and toy soldiers. Roman children had model soldiers in 27 B.C., and flat soldiers of lead were very popular in the eighteenth and nineteenth centuries. In 1893, a British firm invented hollow toy soldiers in place of the flat lead ones which had been imported from Germany. In 1966, plastic began to replace metal. Model vehicles quickly go out of date and are fascinating to collect. Your father's models may now be worth quite a lot of money. You might like to specialize in cars, ships or military vehicles.

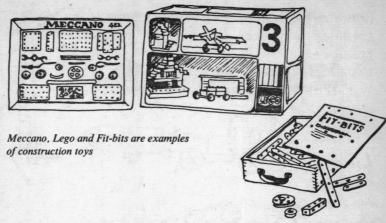

Meccano, Lego and Fit-bits are examples
of construction toys

Mechanical toys also date quickly, and early clockwork models
are becoming rare. Toys from before the 1939 war may still be
around in your house, but even later ones can be different from
your own. Push-along friction vehicles and animals come into this
category too. There is a fine collection of early metal working toys,
called 'penny toys', in the Museum of London.

Many children had to make do with simpler toys, and you
may find interesting ones like yo-yos, cup-and-ball, and diabolo,
which are still made, although there are older ones to be found in
junk shops. If you like decorative things, look for such pretty little
toys as snowstorms or model gardens (see also Dolls' houses). To
give you some idea of the range of toys available, try and visit one

*An old-fashioned flat lead soldier,
a later lead soldier and a plastic one*

or two special museums such as: The Bethnal Green Museum, Cambridge Heath Road, London E2; Cambridge & County Folk Museum, Castle Street, Cambridge; Colchester and Essex Museum, Castle Park, Colchester, Essex; The Museum of London, London Wall, EC2; Museum of Childhood, 38 High Street, Edinburgh; and The Castle Museum, Tower Street, York.

Lace, embroidery and dress trimmings

Often in old needlework baskets, and on junk stalls or at jumble sales, you will find a mixture of buttons, threads, bits of lace, oddments of beadwork and embroidery. When these are sorted out, the pieces of needlework are very pretty to look at and sometimes to use.

Women used to make all sorts of edgings in crochet and tatting, and these are often still attached to handkerchiefs, collars, underwear, tablecloths and mats. A lot of these things were thrown away when they were a bit worn or when more modern and easily

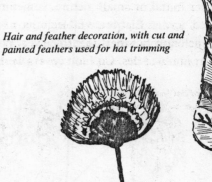

Hair and feather decoration, with cut and painted feathers used for hat trimming

laundered designs became fashionable. Beadwork was another popular occupation, and you can find beaded sleeves or dress fronts among odd pieces of fabric. Sometimes the beads were made into little purses, often for a favourite man, or into flowers for buttonholes or hats. Hats were very elaborately trimmed, and there were fabric flowers as well as bead ones, together with beautiful ribbons and knots of fabric or ribbon, feathers and fruit.

Embroidery was also widely used, particularly for household and table linen. Instead of using woven or printed name tapes, our grandparents used to mark towels and sheets, and even sometimes their clothes, with embroidered initials. Sometimes small pictures in embroidery were used for decoration, and handkerchiefs often had a corner initial or small picture, sometimes matched by an embroidered border. Elaborate tablecloths, mats and napkins are not used much now but they used to be very popular and you can find them at jumble sales. Cushion covers were embroidered too,

Embroidered initials for attaching to clothes and corner initial for a handkerchief

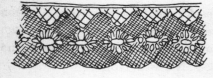

Scalloped edging with sequin and jet decorations, and a delicate lace edging

Fabric heavily decorated in beadwork made with hundreds of tiny beads

Beadwork flowers used as a lapel or hat decoration

often with the addition of a painted or beadwork design. Families used all sorts of things to protect their furniture, such as long runners for tables, sets of mats for dressing tables, and antimacassars to protect chairs from gentlemen's hair oil. These were also made in lace or crochet work, or were embroidered on cloth, and can often be found tucked into drawers or cupboards, or on junk stalls.

137

You can find information on these crafts in books, and pictures of them in old magazines and family pictures. There are also some good collections in museums such as: The American Museum, Claverton Manor, Bath, Avon; Museum of Costume, Assembly Rooms, Bath, Avon; Blaise Castle Folk Museum, Henbury, Bristol, Avon; Honiton Museum, High Street, Honiton, Devon; The Bethnal Green Museum, Cambridge Heath Road, London E2; Victoria & Albert Museum, Cromwell Road, London SW7; Gallery of English Costume, Rusholme, Manchester; and Strangers' Hall, Charing Cross, Norwich, Norfolk.

Bottles and jars

Collecting bottles and jars has become a great craze, and they can be expensive if bought in shops, but it is still possible to find a lot of interesting bottles yourself. They can be found in old rubbish tips, on river beds and in hedges, and of course tucked away at the back

Sauce bottle and wicker-covered lavender-water bottle

of cupboards. Be sure to ask permission if you want to dig on private land, and leave the place tidy afterwards. If you follow the track of an old road which has now returned to grassland, you can find a lot of bottles and jars which were discarded as people walked or rode along.

You can find containers which were used for medicines and ointments, sauces and pickles, ink, glue, vinegar, beer and cider and soft drinks. Some people like to collect only bottles used for

Early jar for children's tonic food, and sweet jar

Wooden stopper for Codd's Wallop bottle which pushed the marble into the neck

Hamilton torpedo bottle which had to be laid on its side

Elaborate bottles for toilet preparations

Early medicine and chemists' bottles

one item, such as ink bottles or soft-drink bottles. Others collect a range of different colours, or bottles made before a certain date. Printed stoneware jars, which are also popular, were used for toiletries, preserves, potted fish and meat, but some of these have been copied in recent years. Often only the lids of these old pots can be found.

Many people are particularly pleased if they find a Codd's Wallop bottle, or a Hamilton torpedo. The first was made in 1875 by Hiram Codd for his soft drinks and has a marble in the twisted neck. If you are very lucky you may also find the wooden presser with which the marble was pushed into the bottle to release the liquid. The Hamilton bottle was invented in 1814 and it has a

Varieties of soft-drink bottles including Codd's Wallop with a coloured marble in the neck

rounded bottom. The bottles had to be put on their sides so the corks were kept moist and the drinks kept fresh and fizzy. These bottles continued in use until the internal screw stopper was invented in 1872.

When you find bottles, let them soak gently in warm soapy water until they are clean. Wipe them very dry and display them on a shelf or window-sill with the light coming through them. Keep a notebook to record where you found each bottle and what you have found out about it. If you want to know more, you can join the British Bottle Collectors' Club, 19 Hambro Avenue, Rayleigh, Essex. There is also a magazine *Bottles & Relics News*, Greenacres, Church Road, Black Notley, Braintree, Essex.

Musical instruments

You probably already know how to play a musical instrument, like a recorder, and if you are interested in music you can make a collection of all sorts of simple instruments. These need not be expensive and are often sold in toy shops and on market stalls or in Indian or African craft shops.

One of the most interesting instruments to collect is the whistle as there are so many different kinds. There are wood and pottery bird whistles, penny whistles and swanee whistles. Other good 'blowing' instruments include recorders, flutes and trumpets, and, of course, mouth organs. There are many kinds of drums, including foreign and toy ones. Xylophones come in many varieties too, and also the small percussion instruments like triangles, gongs and cymbals.

Trumpet and toy drum

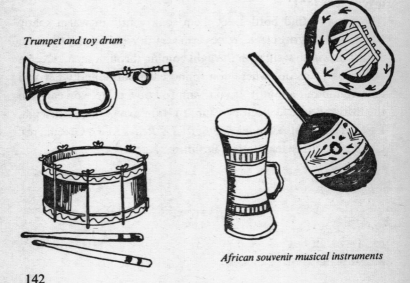

African souvenir musical instruments

Whistles in a variety of shapes are among the earliest musical instruments

Decorative tambourine, a souvenir from Portugal

Flageolet and sopranino recorder are favourite wind instruments

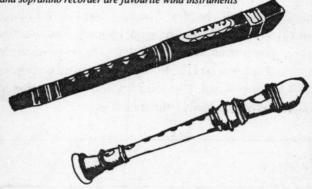

Souvenirs from foreign countries often take the form of musical instruments. There are African rattles and bongo drums, Japanese flutes, South American ocarinas, Indian bells, West Indian maracas, and Spanish tambourines and castanets.

Really old instruments are of course expensive, but sometimes you can find an old zither, banjo or accordion in a junk shop. If you are lucky you may find sheet music to go with them, with very amusing old pictures on it.

143

Austrian bell and Spanish castanets are musical souvenirs

Many museums have collections of musical instruments. Some of the most interesting collections are at: Snowshill Manor, Broadway, Worcestershire; Russell Collection of Harpsichords and Clavichords, Niddry Street, Cowgate, Edinburgh; The Musical Museum, Kew Bridge, Middlesex; Fenton House, The Grove, Hampstead, London NW3; The Horniman Museum, London Road, Forest Hill, London SE23; Royal College of Music, Prince Consort Road, London SW7; and The Bagpipe Museum, St Nicholas Street, Newcastle-upon-Tyne.

Sweets

You probably think that sweets are only for eating, but not long ago there was an exhibition of sweets, showing all the strange shapes in which they can be made. Often they really are too pretty or too amusing to eat, and they are great fun to collect, particularly as sweets are often a nice cheap souvenir from a holiday. Most of these sweets are made in hard sugar, chocolate or marzipan, and they are often packed in unusual boxes too. A lot of the best ones

Liquorice pipe with
hundreds-and-thousands tobacco

Marzipan fruit

Pink candy earrings
imported into England
from Hong Kong

Coconut tobacco and sugar cigarettes

Chocolate fish in box from France

Painters' and workmen's tools modelled
in chocolate or jelly

Marzipan pig and poached eggs from Germany

Hard sugar lollipops with decorative faces, and sugar orange made in segments and wrapped in paper with 'leaves'

Chocolate cat wrapped in printed silver paper

Sailor's hat containing sugar pebbles from France

LE TOUQUET

come from Italy, France and Germany, so perhaps friends or your family can bring some back for you.

Animals and fish are particularly popular made in sweet shapes. Look out for sugar and chocolate mice, sugar and marzipan pigs, and marzipan lambs which commemorate Easter in Italy. In France, they make chocolate sardines in tins, and chocolate oysters in barrels, and even chocolate snails. Sugar shrimps and sugar pebbles are popular at the seaside too, and in France they are packed in boxes which look like sailors' hats. Marzipan vegetables and cooked dishes (such as bacon and eggs) are particularly popular in Germany, and chocolate nuts are often found in France or Italy wrapped to look like hazelnuts or walnuts. In northern France, they like to make sweets look like dairy produce, with nougat wrapped like cream cheese, and pretend Camembert or Brie in cheese boxes. At Easter, eggs are not the only popular shape. Look out for chocolate rabbits, fish and lambs. At Christmas look for chocolate cats, people, clocks, candles and

146

Easter lamb modelled in sugar or marzipan from Italy

Animals, fish and reptiles made in chocolate, jelly or sugar

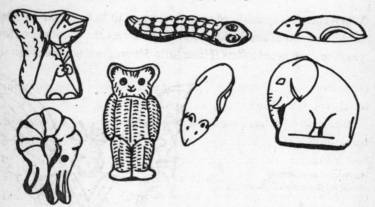

Christmas tree decorations in pretty coloured papers. In France, christenings are celebrated with sugar almonds made to look like boy or girl babies in bonnets, packed in rows like children in bed.

Sweets which look like smokers' things have always been popular. You can find chocolate pipes and cigars, chocolate and sugar cigarettes in many different packets, sugar matches, and coconut tobacco. Lollipops are fun too, but can be breakable. Some are made to look like slices of lemon or orange, or they can be in odd twisted shapes, or look like faces, or have pretty patterns in different colours set into them. At the seaside look for rock

147

made into funny shapes like packets of sausages, sets of teeth, fruit, human legs or babies' bottles.

If you can't resist eating the sweets, you can at least save the containers. Try to find some of the old-fashioned tins of Harrogate toffee or Berwick cockles or other regional sweets which have been packed the same way for over a hundred years. In France they like to pack Montelimar nougat in boxes which look like milestones.

Cake and Christmas decorations

When there's a special occasion, it is usual to bake a cake to celebrate, and some families like to keep the same cake decorations for years or even generations. These little decorations are great fun to

Cracker decoration of artificial flowers and silver bells

Christmas tree fairy

148

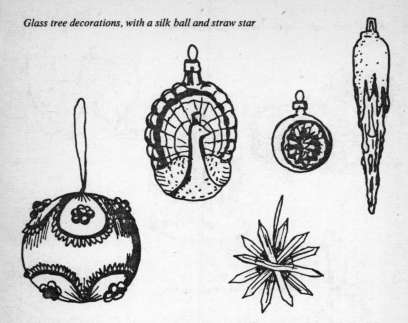

collect and it is amazing how many kinds there are. Christmas cakes may have robins, Eskimoes, holly or trees, and Father Christmas may be on a sledge or a rocket, or walking with a sack or even a teddy bear. Easter brings rabbits and chickens for the cake and there are always birthday fruit, flowers and numbers. Wedding cakes may be decorated with horseshoes and orange blossom, or with a model of a bridal couple, and christening cakes often have little models of cradles or storks.

A lot of cakes have unusual candle holders too. Many of them are flowers made of metal, plastic or sugar icing, but there are also little wooden trains, sets of fairies, ballet dancers, animals, footballers, soldiers and military bands made to hold tiny candles. Another way of celebrating is to decorate a Christmas tree. You are probably used to the coloured glass balls which come in many sizes and shapes, but there are also straw and wood-shaving decorations from Scandinavia, little tin figures from Mexico and glass

149

Easter, christening and Christmas cake decorations

Christmas tree candle holders

birds with shiny tails from Czechoslovakia. If you like other trimmings, look for old-fashioned candle holders, or for different kinds of tinsel. You may also find cut-out paper decorations which extend to chains, or intricately cut paper bells, animals, snowmen or Father Christmasses. You might find elaborate cracker decorations too, as these used to be very expensive and elaborate, and included velvet flowers, model ships and fairy dolls.

Keys and locks

Most families have a bunch of keys, and a lot of keys are no longer used because everyone has forgotten what they belong to. Ask if you can have these and start a collection. Modern keys are standardized and not very interesting, but there are many older ones which are fascinating. There were heavy iron keys made from the seventeenth century onwards, and attractive eighteenth- and nineteenth-century ones made in brass. The eighteenth-century

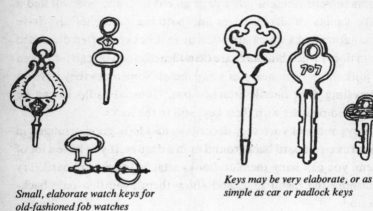

Small, elaborate watch keys for old-fashioned fob watches

Keys may be very elaborate, or as simple as car or padlock keys

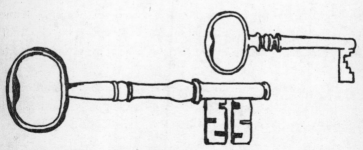

Old door key and cupboard key with large 'bows' or handles

151

keys have a particularly fine 'bow' which is the part you hold to turn. There are door keys of course, but also keys for furniture and small boxes and some of these are very pretty.

The locks in which they turn are also fascinating. Look at all the doors in your house if you live in an old one, and you will find a huge variety of shapes, sizes and patterns. Churches also have fascinating locks which are often huge. Locks are often discarded from doors when buildings are demolished, and you can find them in junk shops or in heaps of scrap metal. Sometimes they have an interesting door handle attached too. Unusual padlocks can be found, sometimes with their keys still in the locks.

Keys and locks are very decorative and look good arranged in patterns on a board background or in a drawer. If you have a lot of them, you can hang them on hooks attached to a peg board. Try polishing the metal first, and show them against a pale background.

Eggs

Eggs are a symbol of spring and of rebirth, and so they have come
to be a sign of hope and good luck. That is why we give eggs at
Easter. Real eggs used to be decorated with wax patterns, dye or
paint. Red patterns commemorate the blood which dripped from
the Cross on Good Friday on to a basket of eggs brought by Mary.
You can often buy pretty decorated eggs which come from the
Ukraine in Russia, and in 1963 there were more than sixty known
designs.

In Russia and other countries of Eastern Europe, these patterns
were also used for carved wooden eggs, and some of these contained tiny nesting eggs. The Russians have always loved pretty
eggs, and a famous jeweller called Fabergé used to make a jewelled
egg each year for the Royal Family. The egg contained a precious
jewel or model (sometimes an animal or a horse-drawn carriage) in

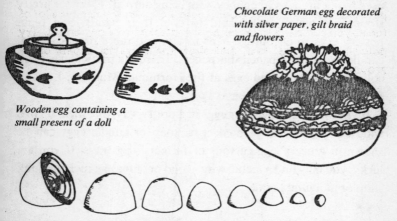

*Chocolate German egg decorated
with silver paper, gilt braid
and flowers*

*Wooden egg containing a
small present of a doll*

*Wooden nesting egg containing different coloured eggs, the smallest being
tinier than a pea*

153

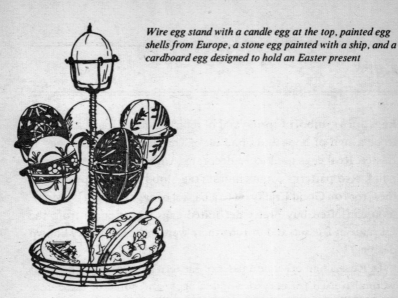

Wire egg stand with a candle egg at the top, painted egg shells from Europe, a stone egg painted with a ship, and a cardboard egg designed to hold an Easter present

gold and rare stones. Today, there are many less valuable eggs which are made to hold little presents. You can find them in wood, china and cardboard, often with a pretty pattern.

If you like egg shapes, look for wooden or stone eggs which were used to put in socks when they were being darned. There are pretty stone eggs which ladies held to cool their hands, and plain pottery eggs to encourage hens to lay, and more practical 'egg' candles, soaps and pencil sharpeners. There is a particularly good collection of decorated eggs at the Horniman Museum, London Road, Forest Hill, London SE23.

If you want to show your eggs in a pretty way, pile them up in a wide bowl. Delicate painted eggs, soap or candle eggs can be shown in grocers' egg cartons or farmers' egg trays. If you are lucky, you may find a metal, wire, wood or china egg rack in a junk shop or at a jumble sale.

Index

Other non-fiction in Puffins

The Big Book of Puzzles   *Michael Holt and Ronald Ridout*
The Boomerang Book   *M. J. Hanson*
Chorus: The Puffin Colony Song Book   *David Green*
Cooking is a Game you can Eat   *Fay Maschler*
Fun with Collage   *Jan Beaney*
Fun with Paper Modelling   *G. C. Payne*
How to Survive   *Brian Hildreth*
The Insects in your Garden   *Harold Oldroyd*
The Junior Puffin Quiz Book   *Norman and Margaret Dixon*
Making a Miniature Village   *Guy R. Williams*
Making Presents and Other Things   *Belinda Price*
The Paper Aeroplane Book   *Seymour Simon*
Paper Folding and Modelling   *Aart van Breda*
Paper World   *Clive Manning*
Puffin Book of Brainteasers   *Eric Emmet*
Puffin Book of Car Games   *D. St P. Barnard*
Puffin Book of Flags   *John George*
Puffin Book of Freshwater Fishing   *Roger Pierce*
Puffin Book of Gardening   *Mary Kelly*
Puffin Book of Magic   *Norman Hunter*
Puffin Crossword Puzzle Book   *Alan Cash*
Puffin Quiz Book   *Norman and Margaret Dixon*
Puffin Soccer Quiz Book   *David Prole*
Puffin Song Book   *compiled by Leslie Woodgate*
Second Big Book of Puzzles   *Michael Holt and Ronald Ridout*
Something to Do   *Septima*
Something to Make   *Felicia Law*
Things to Do   *Hazel Evans*

Heard about the Puffin Club?

... it's a way of finding out more about Puffin
books and authors, of winning prizes (in
competitions), sharing jokes, a secret code, and
perhaps seeing your name in print! When you join
you get a copy of our magazine, *Puffin Post*, sent
to you four times a year, a badge and a
membership book.

For details of subscription and an application
form, send a stamped addressed envelope to:

The Puffin Club Dept A
Penguin Books Limited
Bath Road
Harmondsworth
Middlesex UB7 0DA

and if you live in Australia, please write to:

The Australian Puffin Club
Penguin Books Australia Limited
P.O. Box 257
Ringwood
Victoria 3134